50 Country Garden Cross-Stitch Designs

STEP-BY-STEP

50 Country Garden Cross-Stitch Designs

Lynda Burgess

Photography by Amanda Heywood

SMITHMARK

This edition published in 1996 by
SMITHMARK Publishers, a division of U.S. Media Holdings, Inc.
16 East 32nd Street
New York
NY 10016

SMITHMARK books are available for bulk purchase for sales promotion and for premium use.
For details write or call the manager of special sales, SMITHMARK Publishers Inc. 16 East
32nd Street, New York, 10016; (212) 532 6600

ISBN 1 8317 7284 0

Produced by Anness Publishing Limited
1 Boundary Row
London SE1 8HP

Printed and bound in Hong Kong

CONTENTS

Introduction   6

TECHNIQUES   12

SPRING   20

SUMMER   38

AUTUMN   59

WINTER   76

Index   96

INTRODUCTION

During the seventeenth century, gentlewomen would spend many hours stitching, and the cross stitch subsequently became very popular in sampler work. Later, in the nineteenth century, sewing was a compulsory subject for girls who went to school, and cross stitch was used for marking laundry. Such was the importance of needlework, that young girls could use their stitching skills to secure jobs as maids and housekeepers. With the establishment of the sewing machine, the need for hand-stitching waned during the earlier part of the twentieth century, and interest in decorative needlecrafts took a tumble. In the last twenty years, however, people have once again become enthusiastic about needlecrafts and cross stitch is the most popular because, once mastered, anyone can do it.

Cross stitch is a versatile medium for stitching. It allows you to create unique designs using only a needle and thread. Working from an easy-to-follow chart, even novices can produce elegant pictures to grace their homes. The stitches grow quickly, and you can watch the work develop before your eyes. It is an incredibly satisfying experience and a thrill when you can turn to friends and say "I did that".

Step-by-Step 50 Country Garden Cross-Stitch Designs brings together beautiful country designs that everyone will want to stitch. We have compiled a collection of designs ranging from the simple, quick and easy to more complicated, detailed designs which will challenge even the most accomplished needleworker. The projects have a seasonal theme, with designs for spring, summer, autumn and winter. Each one comes with a chart and key, and for those which need making up, there are step-by-step instructions to guide you through. Inspirational ideas for mounting your work will make you realize how effective cross stitch can be for so many different occasions and have you itching to start stitching!

aida tea towel

evenweave

Materials

The projects in this book have been worked using widely available materials. For a long time colour choices have been limited, but nowadays manufacturers are realising that embroiderers enjoy working on a variety of coloured materials and so are extending their colour ranges. If you can't find the colour you want to use, ask at your local needlecraft-shop.

Chart paper

If you want to adapt or change a chart, chart paper will make your life a lot easier. It comes in a variety of sizes and is transparent, with a grid marked on it. It is useful for marking repeats.

Fabrics

Two types of fabric are mainly used: evenweave and two gauges of aida. The aida is a twin thread fabric where the stitches are worked into every hole; evenweave has even warp and weft threads. The evenweave projects are worked over two threads on a 28 count fabric which makes the equivalent finished size comparable to that of working on a 14hpi aida.

Fabric counts are assessed by the number of holes per inch (hpi). Using a ruler you can measure and count these holes. It will help you to work out the finished size of your piece. The gauge of the fabric will affect the size. The larger the gauge, the finer the work. New stitchers may find a larger gauge tricky to work at first
Aida band: The band is produced in widths from 2.5–7.5 cm (1–3 in). It is an edged length of fabric with an aida strip running through the middle. It can be used for hat bands or shelf edging.
Aida tea towel: As cross stitch grows in popularity, more and more items are being made specially for working your cross stitch. The cotton tea towel is one of them. It has an aida strip along one edge on which you can work a border design.

Felt

Felt is a bonded fabric which is ideal for backing work as it doesn't fray and is firm and easy to handle.

Interfacing

This is a bonded interlining which is used to stiffen and support a fabric. It comes in either iron-on or sew-in form.

Metallic thread

Metallic threads add lustre and detail to your work. The thread is thicker and stiffer than an ordinary embroidery thread and usually comes on spools of a single thread. It is ideal for details.

Plastic canvas

This is a plastic evenweave mesh which comes in a variety of gauges. It is firm and ideal for three-dimensional projects.

Sewing thread

Use sewing thread for making up your projects. You can use either a polyester or cotton thread. Match the thread to the fabric you are using.

Stranded cotton

Stranded cottons are used throughout. These come in skeins of six strands. Cut a length to work with, and split the skein so that you are only working with the number of strands specified for a particular project. The range of colours available is immense.

Waste canvas

If you want to work your cross stitch on to a garment, or any other item which does not have an obvious weave to work from, you can transfer your design by using waste canvas. The canvas is pre-starched. Attach the canvas to the fabric where you want the design and work your cross stitch through the canvas and the fabric. When finished, simply dampen the canvas to remove the starch and gently remove the threads, leaving the design on the fabric.

aida band

aida

chart paper

metallic thread

sewing thread

plastic canvas

felt

stranded cotton

aida

fabrics

interfacing

Equipment

Cross stitch is a portable hobby: once hooked, embroiderers take their work everywhere with them. With this in mind, it may explain why you don't need a lot of equipment – it wouldn't be practical to carry around anyway. However, there are a few essentials you should keep with you at all times.

Beads

To add detail to a design you can thread beads on to your needle and work them in to your cross-stitch design.

Embroidery frame

Working on an embroidery frame keeps the fabric taut and helps reduce any distortion. Remember to remove the work from the frame between sessions, so that the fabric doesn't crease or mark.

Embroidery scissors

These specialist scissors are small and have sharp, pointed blades. The pointed ends are ideal for snipping into stitches.

Fabric-marker pen

Use vanishing fabric-marker pens to outline areas before cutting

Flexihoop (UK only)

For an easy mounting idea, opt for a flexihoop. The rubber outer ring slips off the inside ring. You place your embroidery over the inside ring and reposition the outer ring. Flexihoops come in a variety of types and sizes, and are widely available from most specialist shops.

General-purpose scissors

Use general-purpose scissors for cutting fabric and paper. They are usually larger than embroidery scissors and have more rounded ends.

Glue

If you need to use glue to make up your work, use a general-purpose adhesive which is suitable for fabric. However, if you want your work to last for ever, avoid glue if possible, adding a couple of small stitches instead. Most glues will damage the fabric after a time.

Masking tape

Use masking tape to protect the edges of your embroidery when working. It will help to avoid snagging.

Needles

A selection of needles is vital. For cross stitch, an 18–22 crewel or tapestry needle is ideal. These needles have a large eye and a relatively blunt point. For other embroidery stitches use a sharper needle. If you have a variety of needles loaded with different coloured threads, it will save you time and effort.

Pins

There are a variety of pins to choose from. Stainless steel dressmakers' pins are suitable for most work. If you're working on white fabric, you may like to invest in gold-plated pins which will not rust.

Pinking shears

These scissors have a zig-zag blade and are ideal to use for neatening the edges of your work. The finish minimizes fraying.

Quick unpick (seam ripper)

If you make a mistake when making up your work, use a quick unpick (seam ripper). The V-shaped blade will efficiently cut open a seam in seconds.

Tape measure

A tape measure is a useful accessory: for measuring up your finished work, for cutting your fabric at the outset and for making it up into the finished item.

Thimble

If you want to avoid needle pricks, you can work with a thimble. This is really a matter of preference: some people would rather work without, and suffer the consequences of a few pricked fingers.

flexihoop

embroidery hoop

glue

fabric-marker pen

tape measure

beads

pins

embroidery scissors

brass rings

thimble

needles

general-purpose scissors

uick
npick (seam
pper)

masking tape

pinking shears

TECHNIQUES

Cross stitch

This easy-to-make stitch is used as the basic stitch for all the projects in this book. With a crossing motion, take the thread across the weave into all four corners. You can use cross stitch to create the most beautiful and enduring needlework projects.

Continuous cross stitch

If you're working large areas of a single colour, you may find it more efficient to use a continuous cross stitch. Work a strip of diagonal stitches, turn your needle and come back over the stitches, working the diagonal in the opposite direction.

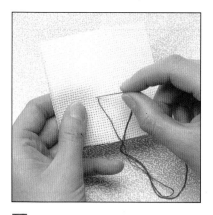

1 Bring your needle up at the bottom corner of a stitch. Take it down into the opposite top corner to form a half cross stitch.

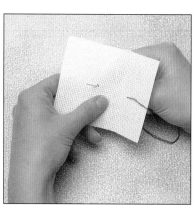

2 Bring it up in the adjacent bottom hole and finish the stitch by taking it down into the opposite top hole.

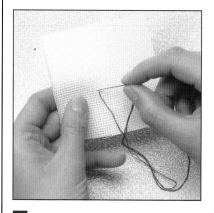

1 Bring your needle up through the fabric at the bottom corner of a stitch. Take it down in the opposite top corner.

2 Repeat this with the next stitch and the following ones, forming a row of half cross stitches.

3 Repeat steps 1 and 2 for a row of stitches.

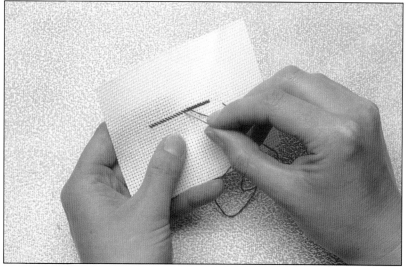

3 When you have completed your row, turn the needle around and complete the stitches, forming the completing row across the first row.

Half stitch

The half stitch is made up of a row of diagonal stitches. You simply form half of the cross stitch. This stitch is used where you want a lighter feel; it can also add texture to your work.

Three-quarter stitch

Working a stitch with two colours helps to add definition to a detailed piece of embroidery. The three-quarter stitch should sit against the heavier area of colour. Always work the three-quarter stitch first and the quarter stitch – in a different colour – second.

1 Bring your needle up through your fabric at the top corner of a stitch. Take it down through the fabric at the opposite bottom corner.

2 Bring your needle up through the fabric at the adjacent top corner of a stitch, and down again into the opposite corner

1 With the first colour make a half cross stitch.

2 Work as if to complete a full stitch but take the needle into the middle instead of the hole at the opposite side.

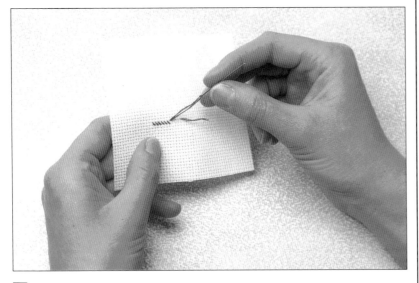

3 Repeat steps 1 and 2 to form a row of half cross stitches.

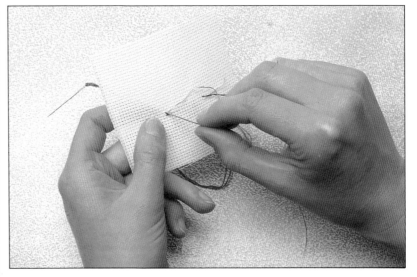

3 With the second colour work the other quarter stitch, bringing it up through the fourth corner to the centre to meet the first quarter stitch worked.

Back stitch

To add detail and definition to your work, back stitch is often used. It is a dense, straight stitch which creates a solid outline around a design.

Holbein stitch

The holbein stitch adds detail too. It is worked as a running stitch into every other hole, and then the needle is reversed and the gaps are filled in – working into the alternate stitches.

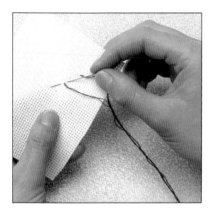 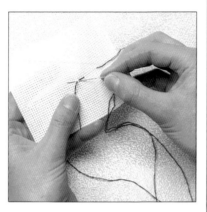 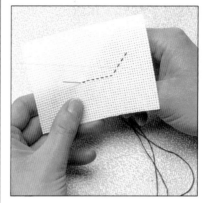 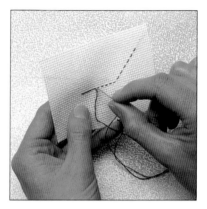

1 Bring needle up one stitch length ahead of where you wish to begin. Drop it into the previous hole, bringing it up again two stitch lengths ahead.

2 Repeat this step, taking the needle back one stitch length and bringing it back up two stitch lengths ahead.

1 Bring your needle up through the fabric where you want to start your outline and stitch a running stitch into every other hole.

2 When you have completed your outline, turn the needle and use a running stitch to fill in the alternate blank spaces.

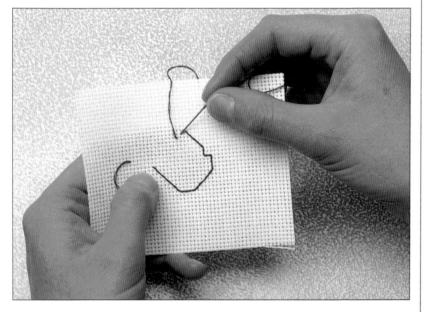 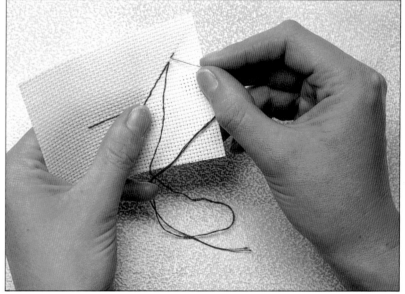

3 Should you wish to turn a corner, bring the needle up into the opposite corner, two stitch lengths ahead and continue stitching as above.

3 To finish off, complete the last running stitch, turn the work to the back and thread the needle back through a few of the stitches before cutting the thread.

Long stitch

Working over several stitch lengths at once, a long stitch is ideal for creating grass or flower stems. Do not work over more than four or five threads, as the stitch may start to loop.

French knots

Texture and dimension can be given to your work by using French knots. The knot is a traditional embroidery stitch which complements cross-stitch designs beautifully.

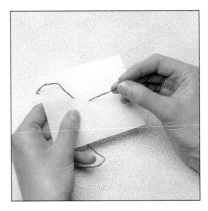

1 Bring your needle up through the fabric where you want the stitch to begin.

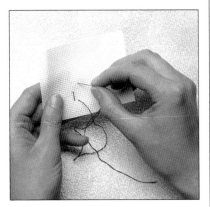

2 Take the needle across the area of your proposed stitches and drop it into the hole where you want the stitch to end.

1 Bring the needle up through the fabric where you want the stitch to be.

2 Make a small stitch and as you bring the needle back through the fabric wrap the end of the thread – nearest to the fabric – twice around the needle.

3 Repeat this action for subsequent stitches, varying the length as necessary. Do not pull the stitches too tight.

3 Pull the needle through these threads, fixing the stitch by taking the needle back through the same hole where it started.

Lacing a picture

Many people will mount their work flat and glue it to a backing board before framing. This is not a good idea. First, if you flatten your stitching you will not show its beauty to its full potential, and secondly, some glues will ruin your work. Use wadding (batting), and lace your work to a board before framing, to give it an elegant look and lasting finish.

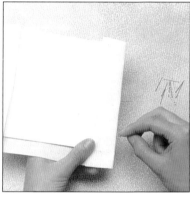

1 Cut some mount board (backing board) to size. Cut a peice of wadding (batting) smaller than the board. Ensure the embroidery is larger than both.

2 Lay the embroidery face down, with the wadding (batting) and the board on top. Wrap the embroidery over the board and pin it to the board's edges.

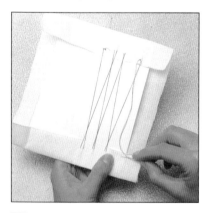

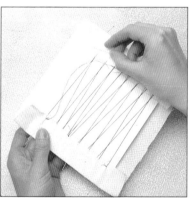

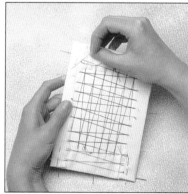

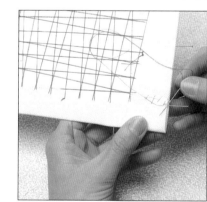

3 By stitching from the middle to the outer edge, start lacing towards the top of the work.

4 Repeat from the middle to the bottom, pulling the thread taut as you move along the edge.

5 Starting from the middle on the adjacent sides, lace the remaining two sides.

6 Turn in the corners and oversew them together. Then neaten all the edges by cutting off the stray threads with a pair of scissors.

Decorating a pot

Pots with hand-stitched tops recall more gracious times when a lady's boudoir contained several powder bowls and trinket boxes. These elegant pots make superb gifts for friends to keep and treasure for ever.

1 Draw around the pot lid on to the wrong side of the embroidery, centring the design in the middle of the pot lid.

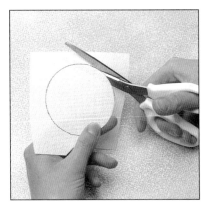

2 Cut around this line leaving a circular or oval shape with your design in the middle.

3 Draw around the wadding (batting) in the same way.

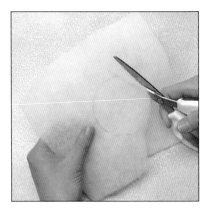

4 Cut the wadding (batting) to the same size.

5 Place the embroidery and the wadding (batting) face down in the lid.

6 Secure your design by fixing with the metal disc.

Filling a card

There are a variety of ways to mount your work
One of the easiest and most useful is in a card.
Aperture cards (with open spaces) are readily
available from craft and needlework shops.

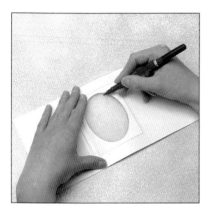

1 Place some wadding (batting) inside the wrong side of the aperture (opening). Draw around it with a marker pen.

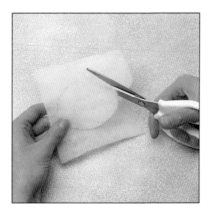

2 Cut the wadding (batting) to the same size as the aperture (opening) on your card.

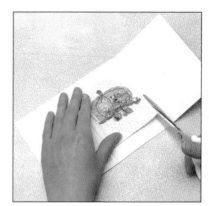

3 Cut down your embroidery to fit the middle section of the card.

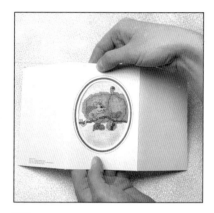

4 Centre the design in the card, face down, so that the design is looking out through the aperture (opening).

5 Place the wadding (batting) behind the aperture (opening) so that it fills adding bulk behind the design.

6 Stick the back section of the card to the middle with glue, adjusting the design to fit neatly as you do so.

Making a bookmark

Projects with a visible back and front need a properly finished back. A bookmark is a prime example of a project which needs this treatment. Use these easy step-by-step instructions to discover how you can give your work a truly professional finish.

1 Measure a piece of felt slightly smaller than the size of your bookmark.

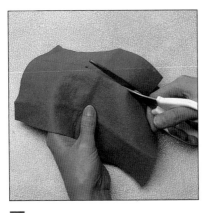

2 Cut the felt to size, taking care that the finished piece comes just inside the edges of the bookmark.

3 Pin the felt to the back of your work.

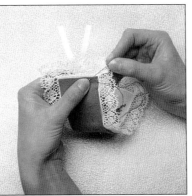

4 Using a small stitch, oversew (slip stitch) the felt, taking care the stitches don't show on the right side.

USING THE CHARTS

Each symbol on the chart represents one stitch. Parts of the design may be outlined in back stitch, this is identified by the solid heavy lines around or through the symbols. The colour for the back stitch detail is included in the instructions. The key tells you which colour strand of cotton to use for each area. Because different manufacturer's threads are not exact equivalents, we have simply given you the colours. Other stitches such as French knots are included in the instructions.

Finally, the stitch count gives you the finished size of your design: the first number is the height and the second the width.

Posy of pansies

Giving a card to someone you love reminds them how much you care. Make this floral posy as a special gift.

MATERIALS
fabric: 14 hpi aida, 13 x 16 cm
   (5 x 6 ½ in)
stranded cotton, as listed in key
needle
scissors
glue
wadding (batting)
fabric-marker pen
card with aperture

1 Work the cross stitch, beginning at the centre of the design. Use two strands of stranded cotton for all the cross stitch.

2 Once all the cross stitch is complete, use one strand of stranded cotton to create outlines in back stitch. Outline the pansies, bow, doily and "faces" of pansies in very light violet; the pansy detail in lemon and the leaf and stem outlines in hunter green.

3 Neatly finish the work and mount the finished work in a greetings card following the instructions on page 18.

card

scissors

needle

wadding (batting)

fabric-marker pen

fabric

stranded cotton

key

⅂ light lemon

– lemon

I green grey

II mid blue violet

+ very light violet

⋉ beige

back stitch: hunter green,
very light violet, lemon

stitch count 41 x 61

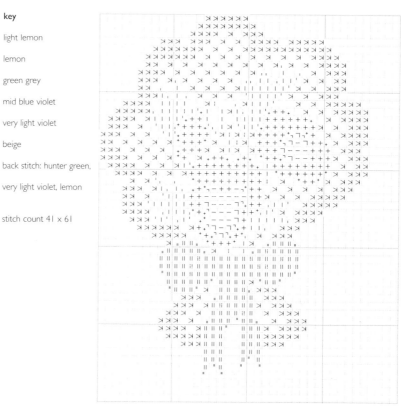

Birds in the bath

Spring brings with it the first birds out looking for food. Along with the first signs of colour and new growth, the birds symbolizes the beginnings of a new season.

MATERIALS
fabric: 28 hpi evenweave over two threads, 10 x 10 cm (4 x 4 in)
stranded cotton, as listed in key
needle
mount board (backing board)
scissors
fabric-marker pen
wadding (batting)
pins
thread
oval frame

1 Work the cross stitch using two strands of stranded cotton for the bird, birdbath and grass. Use one strand for the remainder of the cross stitch.

2 Using one strand, back stitch dark brown grey around the birdbath. Back stitch the beak and legs of the black bird with two strands of dark lemon. Use two strands of dark lemon wrapped once around the needle for the eye. Use two strands of white wrapped twice around the needle for random French knots on the grass, to represent daisies.

3 Lace the work, following the instructions on page 16, and frame in an oval frame.

oval frame

stranded cotton

wadding (batting)

fabric-marker pen

scissors

needle

fabric

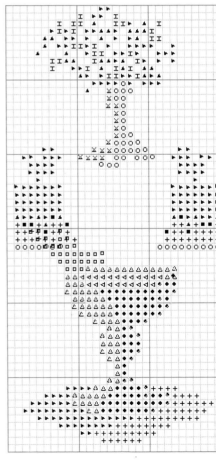

key

△	mid grey
▲	dusky rose pink
I	rose pink
◁	turquoise
▶	yellow leaf green
●	pearl grey
⌣	deep mocha
+	dusky yellow
■	sunshine yellow
□	black

back stitch: dark

brown grey, dark

lemon, white

stitch count 31 x 61

Spring cushion

Delicate blooms start to show after the harsh winter weather passes. Pushing through the soil, the first flowers of spring are a welcome reminder that the warmer weather is on its way.

1 Work the cross stitch using two strands of stranded cotton.

2 Back stitch detail using one strand of stranded cotton on the flowers (*mid left*) in dark raspberry; on the leaf detail (*top right*) in dark forest green. Back stitch the detail on all the pink flowers using two strands of grey; on the stems (*top left*) using two strands of mid sage green and on the flower details (*top right*) using two strands of deep rose. Stitch French knots in light blue randomly around the small blue flowers (*top and bottom left and bottom right*).

MATERIALS
fabric: 14 hpi aida, 35 x 35 cm
  (14 x 14 in)
stranded cotton, as listed in key
needles
thimble
pins
scissors
tape measure
fabric-marker pen
thread
contrasting fabric for cushion
cushion pad
braid trim

contrasting fabric

tape measure

thread

fabric-marker pen

scissors

thimble

needles

stranded cotton

pins

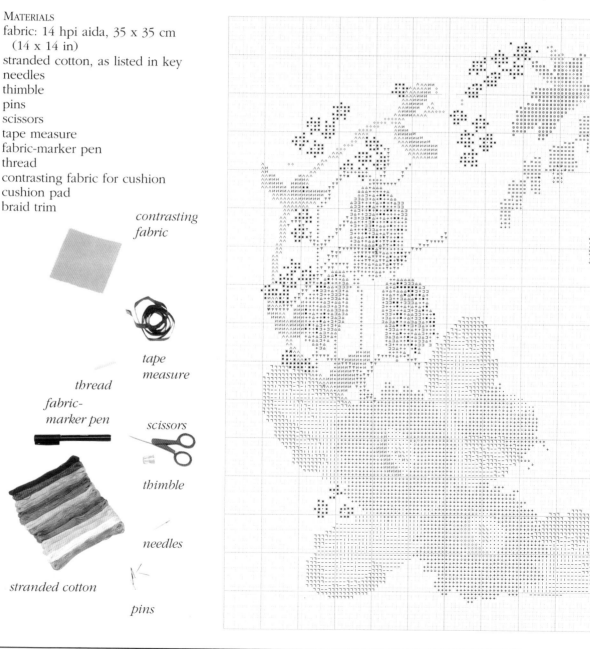

3 Neatly finish off the work before making into a cushion. To complete the cushion, cut four strips of contrasting fabric 8 cm (3 in) wide to border the cross stitch. Stitch the border around the design, sewing the shorter length to the sides first, and then the longer ones to the bottom. Cut a backing in the contrasting fabric the same size as the finished front piece. With right sides together, sew around the edges, leaving an opening to insert the cushion pad. Turn the design through to the right side. Insert the pad and slip stitch the opening shut. Add braid trim.

key

✳	light blue	back stitch: dark rasp-
•	pale yellow	berry, dark forest
◿	dark yellow	green, grey, mid sage
⅂	bright grass green	green, deep rose, light
–	mid grass green	blue
⎮	dark grass green	
+	dark rose pink	
∓	light rose pink	
∧	dark sage green	
⋈	light sage green	
⊐	mid sage green	
■	deep rose	
↑	bright forest green	
→	light forest green	
△	cream	
▽	leaf green	
←	bright leaf green	
↓	dark raspberry	
▢	dusky pink	
○	light dusky pink	
▤	dark dusky pink	
◇	light raspberry	

Bird bookmark

You'll never lose your page again once you've made this decorative bookmark. The appearance of the blue tit (blue bird) tapping away at a milk bottle is a sure sign that spring is really here.

YOU WILL NEED

MATERIALS
fabric: bookmark, 18 hpi aida
  8 x 18 cm (3 x 7 in)
stranded cotton, as listed
  in key
needle
scissors
felt
ruler
fabric-marker pen
pins
threads

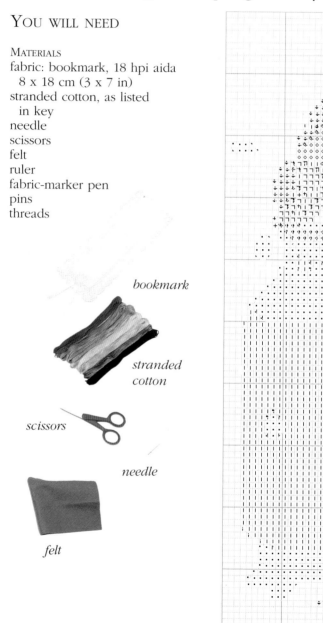

bookmark

*stranded
cotton*

scissors

needle

felt

key

•	flesh
⌐	black
I	white
+	deep grey
⊪	mid grey
⋶	periwinkle blue
⋉	mid royal blue
⊠	pale yellow
○	pale green

back stitch: black, dark grey

stitch count 31 x 101

1 Work the cross stitch using one strand throughout.

2 Add back stitch details in one strand of black for the black facial marking, and deep grey for all other outlines marked on the chart.

3 Neatly finish the work and make into a bookmark following the instructions on page 19.

First snowdrops

Emerging through the new-fallen snow, the snowdrop peeks its delicate head, bringing with it a promise of new life and rich potential for the new year.

YOU WILL NEED

MATERIALS
fabric: 28 hpi evenweave over two threads, 11 x 13 cm (4 ½ x 5 in)
stranded cotton, as listed in key
needle
fabric-marker pen
tape measure
scissors
wadding (batting)
oval pot

1 Work the cross stitch using two strands throughout.

2 Back stitch the detail marked on the chart using one strand of mid parrot green.

3 Neatly finish the work and place in an oval pot following the instructions on page 17.

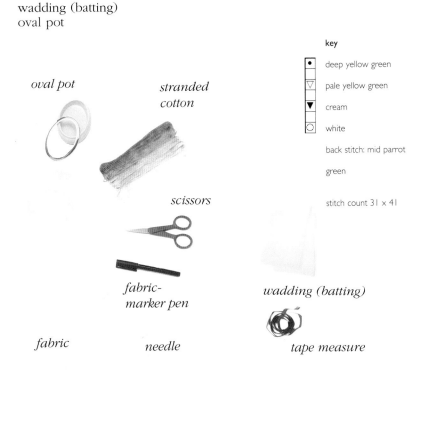

oval pot

stranded cotton

scissors

fabric-marker pen

wadding (batting)

fabric

needle

tape measure

key

●	deep yellow green
▽	pale yellow green
▼	cream
○	white

back stitch: mid parrot green

stitch count 31 x 41

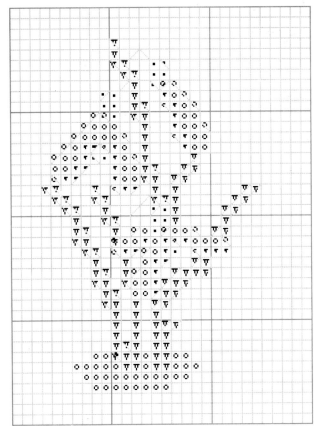

Nightgown case

Keep your nightgown neat and clean in this fresh and elegant case. Simply stitch the design and with a little know-how, turn it into a practical and attractive holdall.

1 Work the cross stitch in two strands throughout.

2 Back stitch the following details in one strand throughout. Gold for the buttercup and primrose; white for the snowdrop; charcoal for one butterfly and blue grey for the other butterfly.

YOU WILL NEED

MATERIALS
fabric: 14 hpi aida (light blue)
  23 x 29 cm (9 x 12 in)
stranded cotton, as listed
  in key
needles
backing fabric
tape measure
fabric-marker pen
scissors
pins
thread
wadding (batting)
3 snap fasteners

wadding (batting)

fabric

lining fabric

pins

scissors

thread

stranded cotton

needles

tape measure

key

•	primrose yellow
ꓶ	deep primrose yellow
—	gold
I	very deep olive green
II	olive green
+	light olive green
╬	dark moss green
☲	mid moss green
⊠	light moss green
⊠	white
∧	black
✳	lilac
I	deep mauve
●	mauve
■	deep cornflower
⊠	mauve blue
←	light gold
↓	lemon
⊥	bright yellow
○	deep yellow
⠿	light leaf green
⊠	mid leaf green
⊡	dark leaf green

back stitch: gold, white,

charcoal, blue grey

stitch count 101 x 131

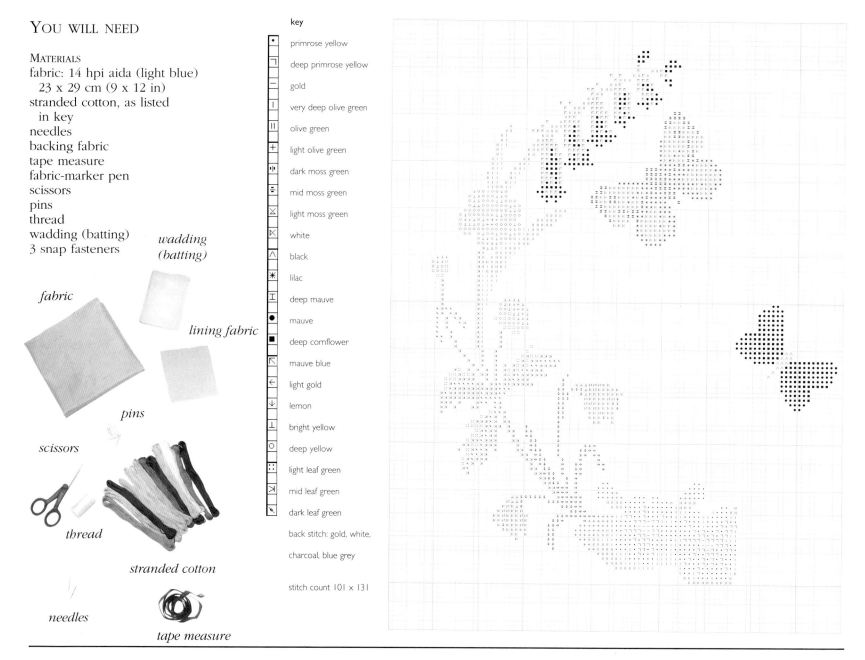

MAKING-UP INSTRUCTIONS

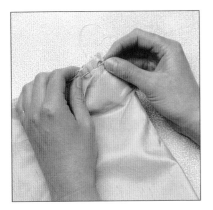

1 Leave a four-row border around the embroidery and attach 8 cm (3 in) wide strips of backing fabric, at least 8 cm (3 in) longer at each end than the embroidered panel. Mitre the corners by folding two adjacent edges together across the corner, right sides together. Stitch from the corner of the embroidery to the outside edge of the border at an angle of 45 degrees. Repeat for all four corners. Attach the wadding (batting) to the back of the work by tacking (basting) around the inside edge of the front panel.

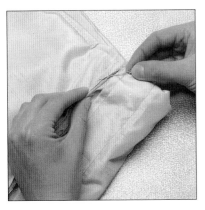

2 Cut backing to the same size as panel and edging stripts. Tack (baste) the backing fabric, right sides together, to the embroidered panel, leaving a gap: you now have the embroidered layer, the wadding (batting) and the backing. Turn to the right side and press. Fold the top edge of the backing fabric under 1.5 cm (⅝ in) and press.

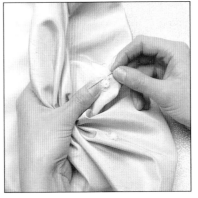

3 Turn under the top edge of front facing of bag 1.5 cm (⅝ in) and stitch in place With right sides together, sew along the edges and bottom of the bag section. Turn to the right side and press. Take the embroidered panel and the bag section right sides together, the back of the bag against the front of the embroidered panel and stitch the raw edge at the top of the bag. Slip stitch the inside edge enclosing all the seams. Sew three snap fasteners at the lower edge of the flap.

Spring cottage

The cottage garden offers rich pickings for flower lover and embroiderer alike. With pastel florals and colourful backgrounds, this cottage environment creates a perfect picture.

1 Work the cross stitch using two strands throughout.

2 Back stitch the detail as marked on the chart, with one strand of black.

3 Neatly finish off the work and lace it, following the instructions on page 16, and frame.

YOU WILL NEED

MATERIALS
fabric: 30 hpi evenweave over
  two threads, 26 x 20 cm (10 x
  8 in)
stranded cotton, as listed in key
needle
mount board (backing board)
tape measure
fabric-marker pen
scissors
wadding (batting)
pins
threads

stranded cotton

fabric

scissors

fabric-marker pen

needle

tape measure

wadding (batting)

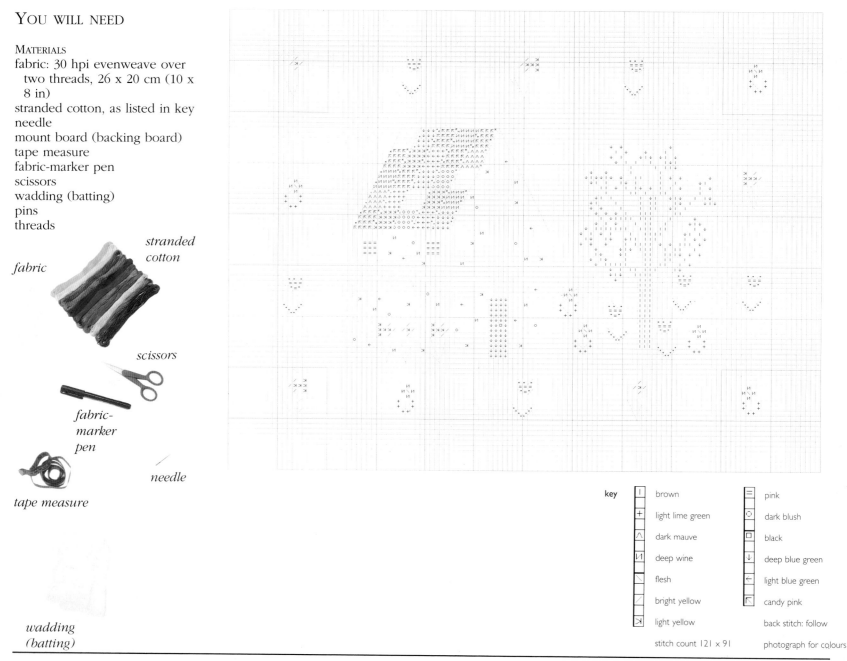

key				
I	brown	☰	pink
+	light lime green	○	dark blush
∧	dark mauve	□	black
И	deep wine	↓	deep blue green
	flesh	←	light blue green
/	bright yellow	⌐	candy pink
⋈	light yellow		back stitch: follow
			photograph for colours

stitch count 121 x 91

Blossom tree

Pale pinks and pastel greens bring the blossom tree to life. Delicate shades of emerging colour create a profusion of beauty unique to this time of year.

YOU WILL NEED

MATERIALS

fabric: 28 hpi evenweave over
  two threads, 10 x 10 cm (4 x
  4 in)
stranded cotton, as listed in key
needle
scissors
fabric-marker pen
crystal (glass) frame

1 Work the cross stitch using two strands throughout.

2 Neatly complete the work. Cut the design to fit the frame using the aperture (opening) of the frame as a guide for size.

*crystal (glass)
frame*

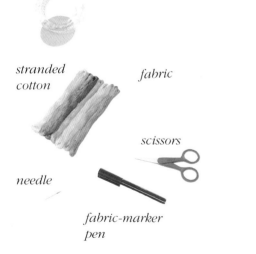

*stranded
cotton*

fabric

scissors

needle

*fabric-marker
pen*

key

	light beige brown
●	medium beige brown
◌	very light cranberry
⌐	light baby pink
+	cranberry
◁	light pine green
▶	very light avocado green

stitch count 31 x 31

Baby fawn

With the spring comes the new – new plants, new flowers and new animals. The fragile fawn, newly born and finding its feet, evokes wonderful memories of the season to come.

YOU WILL NEED

MATERIALS
fabric: 28 hpi evenweave over two threads, 12.5 x 12.5 cm (5 x 5 in)
stranded cotton, as listed in key
needle
scissors
fabric-marker pen
wadding (batting)
round pot

1 Work the cross stitch using two strands for the deer and also for the half cross stitch on the foreground scenery. Cross stitch the background foliage using one strand.

2 Back stitch the details marked on the chart using one strand in the following colours: deep beige for facial features; deep brown for outlining the deer; leaf green for the foliage and mid leaf green for the foreground greenery. Use one strand of white, twisted twice around the needle, for French knots for the eyes.

3 Neatly finish off the work and mount in the round pot following the instructions on page 17.

round pot

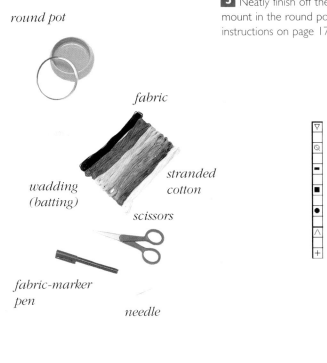

fabric

wadding (batting)

stranded cotton

scissors

fabric-marker pen

needle

key

▽	light beige brown
◲	mid beige brown
−	very light beige brown
■	green grey
●	black
∧	light yellow green
+	white

back stitch: deep beige, deep brown, leaf green, mid leaf green

stitch count 41 x 41

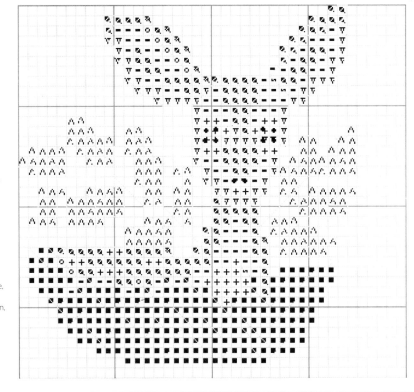

Love cushion

Finding the perfect token to express your love can often be difficult. This sentimental love cushion says it all.

YOU WILL NEED

MATERIALS
fabric: 28 hpi evenweave over
  two threads, 20 cm x
  21.5 cm (8 x 8 ½ in)
stranded cotton, as listed in key
needles
backing material
tape measure
fabric-marker pen
scissors
pins
thread
wadding (batting)
78 cm (31 in) length of 3 cm
  (1¼ in) white lace

*wadding
(batting)*

*backing
material*

thread

*tape
measure*

lace

scissors

fabric

stranded cotton

needle

pins

1 Work the cross stitch using two strands throughout.

2 Back stitch the following details in one strand: dark grey for the dove and flower outline; dark charcoal for the eyes and deep pink for the letters. Back stitch using two strands of the following: grass green for the single flower stems and moss green for the other flower stems.

key

•	deep pink
◺	light pink
⊐	moss green
⌶	pale peach
+	white
⊞	beige
⊟	off white
∧	pale blue
И	light yellow
⋉	grass green
▲	dark charcoal

back stitch: dark grey,
dark charcoal, deep
pink, grass green,
moss green

stitch count 81 x 91

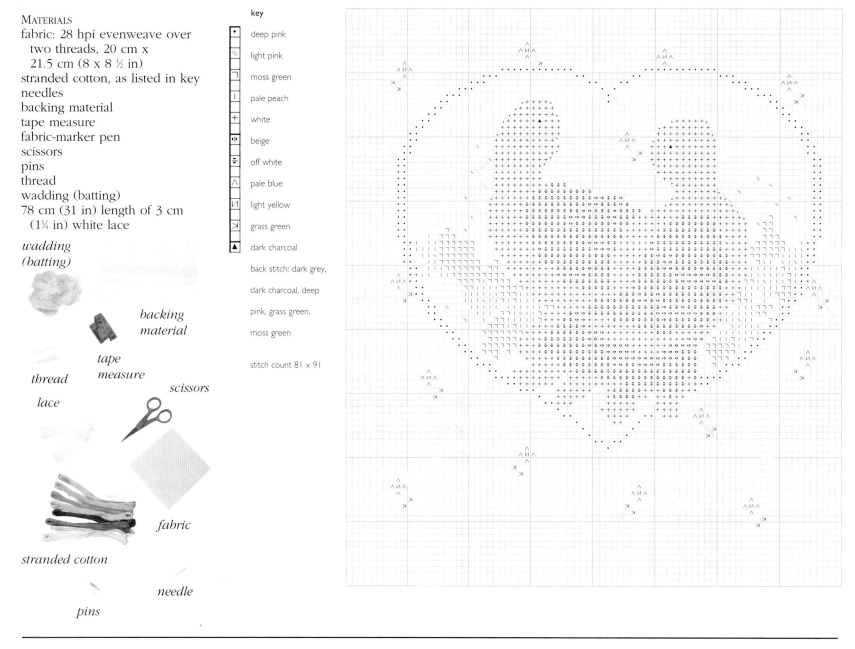

MAKING-UP INSTRUCTIONS

1 Make a cushion pad: cut two 18 cm (7 ¼ in) squares of fabric. Stitch around three sides .5 cm (¼ in) in from the edge. Turn to the right side, fill with wadding (batting), slip stitch fourth side.

2 Stitch a running thread near the edge of the lace and gather up.

3 Sew this to the right side of the backing material leaving a .5 cm (¼ in) margin. Take the embroidery, make a .5 cm (¼ in) hem along each side and press on the wrong side. Oversew (slip stitch) to the backing material. Where the lace and embroidery meet, sew another piece of lace .5 cm (¼ in) wide. Put both parts of the backing material right sides together and stitch along three sides .5 cm (¼ in) from the edge. Turn right sides out, insert the cushion pad and sew up the remaining side.

ALPHABET KEY

Spring sampler

A sampler provides a stitched record of a specific time. Remember a special time by marking the occasion with this original memento of the colours of spring.

YOU WILL NEED

MATERIALS
fabric: 28 hpi evenweave over
   two threads, 30 x 33 cm (12 x
   13 in)
stranded cotton, as listed in key
needle
mount board (backing board)
tape measure
fabric-marker pen
scissors
wadding (batting)
frame
pins
thread

fabric

stranded cotton

wadding (batting)

needle

scissors

tape measure

fabric-marker pen

1 Work the cross stitch using two strands throughout.

2 Work the back stitch detail, using one strand throughout, in the following colours: charcoal for butterfly outlines and antennae; deep pink for the tulip; bright yellow for daffodil; dark yellow for daffodil trumpet; deep periwinkle for grape hyacinth and deep primrose yellow for primrose detail.

3 Work the daffodil stamen in long stitch in one strand of deep yellow. Use two strands for the letters in cross stitch and one strand for the back stitch, all in periwinkle blue.

4 Neatly finish the work. Lace, following the instructions on page 17, and frame.

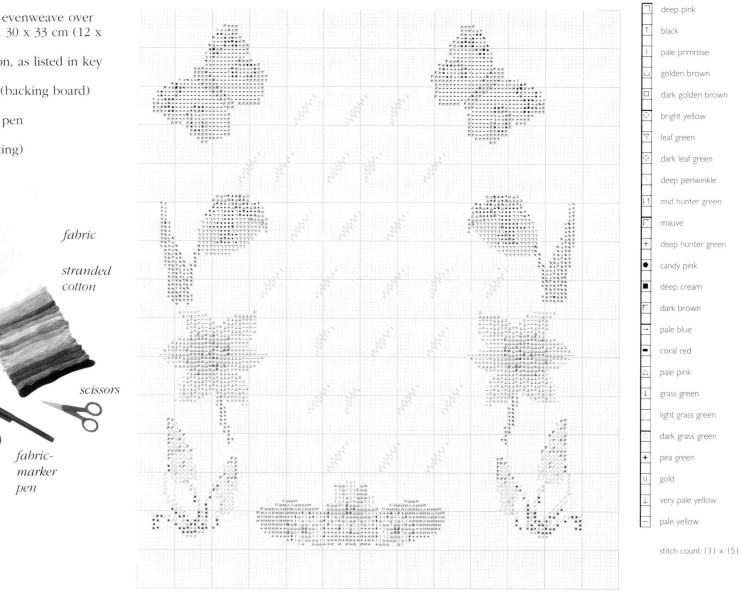

key

⟍	deep pink
↑	black
╵	pale primrose
⊔	golden brown
▯	dark golden brown
⊙	bright yellow
▽	leaf green
⊘	dark leaf green
	deep periwinkle
|↑	mid hunter green
Γ	mauve
+	deep hunter green
●	candy pink
■	deep cream
⌐	dark brown
→	pale blue
▬	coral red
△	pale pink
↓	grass green
	light grass green
◇	dark grass green
✦	pea green
‖	gold
⊥	very pale yellow
—	pale yellow

stitch count 131 x 151

BUTTERFLY DETAIL

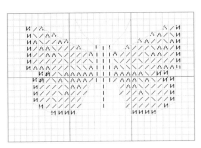

Position the butterfly centrally on the sampler. It is stitched "straddling" the squares. See main chart for positioning.

Butterfly key

I	dark grey
∧	mauve
I1	mauve/white
	mid mauve
	mid mauve/white

back stitch for main design:

deep yellow, periwinkle blue

charcoal, deep pink, bright

yellow, deep periwinkle,

deep primrose

Daffodil doorstop

Rich vibrant yellows can be found in abundance when daffodils bloom; with their deep-hued trumpets and paler leaves, they lend a cheerfulness to every home.

YOU WILL NEED

MATERIALS
fabric: 14 hpi aida, 16 x 27 cm
  (6 ¼ x 10 ¾ in)
stranded cotton as listed in key
needles
brick
wadding (batting)
tape measure
scissors
thread
pins
scissors
velvet

1 Work the cross stitch using two strands throughout.

2 Back stitch the details as marked on the chart, using one strand for each of the following colours: dark orange for the flower centres; medium brown for the main petals (outside markings); bright yellow for the main petals (inside markings); dark green for the leaves and stems; medium brown for the brown stems (calyx).

3 Use two strands for the French knots in the centre of each trumpet using pale yellow thread.

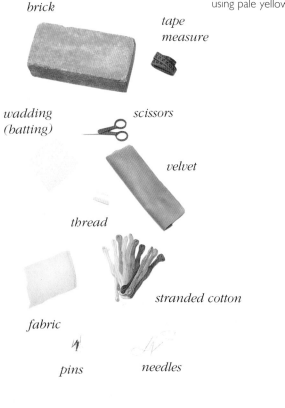

brick

tape measure

wadding (batting)

scissors

velvet

thread

stranded cotton

fabric

pins

needles

key	
⅂	pale yellow
−	bright yellow
I	lemon yellow
II	pale peach
+	peach
◄►	mid yellow orange
⁝	pale yellow orange
⋈	deep yellow orange
⋉	very deep green
◇	yellow green
○	leaf green

back stitch: dark orange,

medium brown, bright

yellow, dark green

stitch count 61 x 121

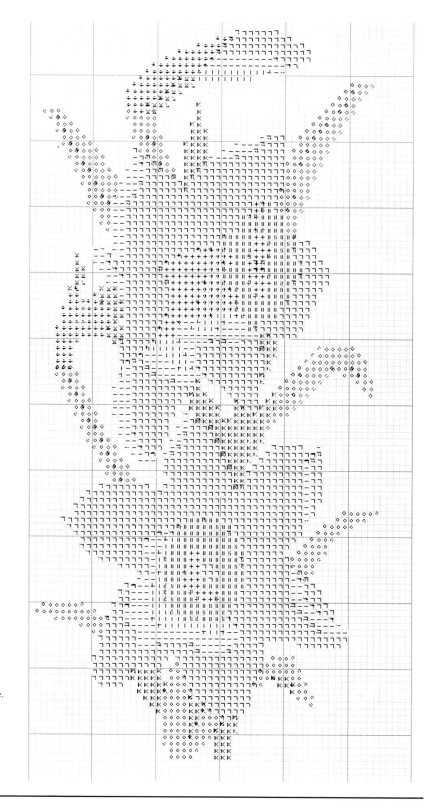

MAKING-UP INSTRUCTIONS

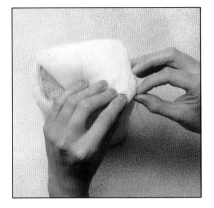

1 Cover the brick with wadding (batting) and tack (baste). Attach 10 cm (4 in) wide velvet strips along each edge of the design allowing 2.5 cm (1 in) extra.

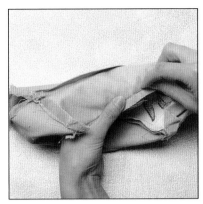

2 With 1.5 cm (½ in) seam allowances, stitch the four velvet strips to the edges of the design, right sides together. Join the side seams.

3 Slip the cover over the brick so that all the edges are covered. Tack (baste) the final piece of velvet to the wide bottom of the brick, covering the bottom and slightly over the edges.

4 Turn under the edges of the cover and slip stitch it to the velvet covering the bottom of the brick.

Poppy doorplate

A doorplate keeps fingerprints at bay. By enclosing an attractive embroidery inside you can add decoration in a practical way.

YOU WILL NEED

MATERIALS
fabric: 14 hpi aida, 11 x 29 cm
  (4½ x 12 in)
stranded cotton, as listed in key
needle
scissors
doorplate with transparent front
backing card (cardboard)

doorplate

fabric

needle

scissors

stranded cotton

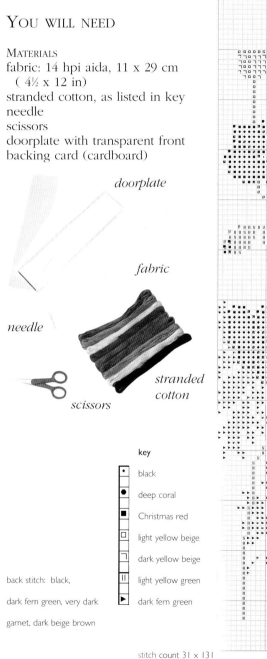

key

·	black
●	deep coral
■	Christmas red
□	light yellow beige
⌐	dark yellow beige
‖	light yellow green
▶	dark fern green

back stitch: black,

dark fern green, very dark

garnet, dark beige brown

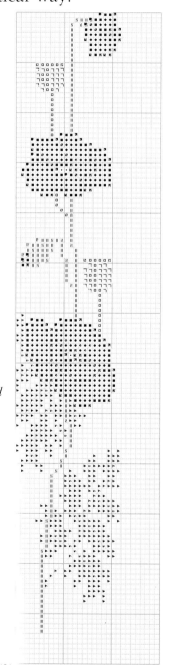

stitch count 31 x 131

1 Work the cross stitch using two strands throughout.

2 Back stitch the details, using one strand in each of the following colours: black for centres and stamens of poppies; very dark garnet for outlining poppy petals; dark fern green for leaves and flower stems; dark beige brown for seed heads and stalks of seed heads.

3 Neatly finish the work. Cut the design to the same size as the doorplate, place behind the plate with the design facing through the glass, and secure in place with a piece of backing card (cardboard) cut to the same size as the doorplate.

Garden card

With the sun shining relentlessly down on your garden, who can blame the bird looking for a refreshing drink? Stitch this card for your favourite garden enthusiast.

YOU WILL NEED

MATERIALS
fabric: 18 hpi aida, 11 x 12 cm
 (4½ x 5 in)
stranded cotton, as listed in key
needle
wadding (batting)
greetings card with aperture
 (opening)
fabric-marker pen
scissors
glue

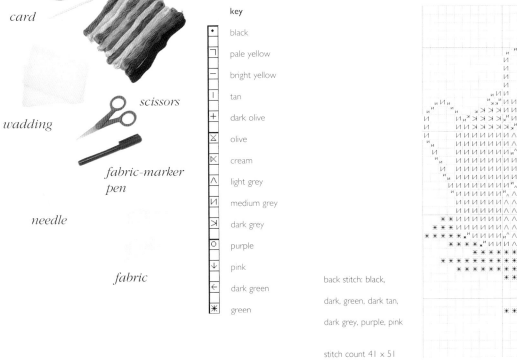

stranded cotton

card

scissors

wadding

fabric-marker pen

needle

fabric

1 Work the cross stitch using two strands throughout.

2 Back stitch the detail, using one strand, for each of the following colours: black for the face and wing outlines; dark green for the bird and leaf outline; dark tan for the beak and legs; dark grey for the can; purple for the flower petals; pink for the flower centre and use two strands of dark green for the flower stems.

3 Neatly finish the work and mount in a greetings card following the instructions on page 18.

key

•	black
⌐	pale yellow
—	bright yellow
I	tan
+	dark olive
⊠	olive
⋉	cream
∧	light grey
И	medium grey
⋈	dark grey
○	purple
↓	pink
←	dark green
✳	green

back stitch: black, dark, green, dark tan, dark grey, purple, pink

stitch count 41 x 51

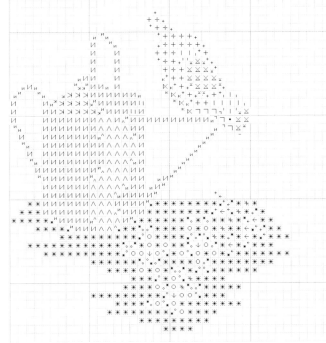

Summer cushion

Garlands of summer flowers spring from this
bright and cheerful design. It's a fabulous project
for an experienced needleworker who is looking
for a challenge.

YOU WILL NEED

MATERIALS
fabric: 14hpi aida, 35 x 35 cm
  (14 x 14 in)
stranded cotton, as listed in key
needle
contrasting fabric for cushion
tape measure
fabric-marker pen
scissors
pins
thread
thimble
cushion pad

fabric

needle

*fabric-marker
pen*

*tape
measure*

scissors

thimble

pins

stranded cotton

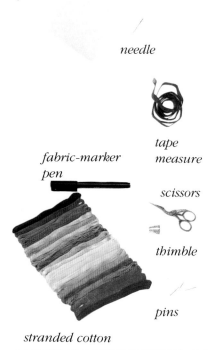

key

•	black
⟋	mid grey
⅂	pale grey
–	dark brown
+	red brown
⊪	fawn
⊟	deep cadmium
⊠	primrose
⊠	Naples yellow
И	eau de nil
⋈	bright light green
∷	grass green
○	dark green
↓	bright blue
←	ultramarine
△	purple
⌐	lilac
→	dark maroon pink
↑	light maroon
▲	fuchsia
✦	candy pink
⊓	flesh
■	scarlet
◁	orange

back stitch: dark purple, fuchsia,

black

stitch count 171 x 171

1 Begin the cross stitch at the centre of the design and work the cross stitch in two strands throughout.

2 Back stitch details, using one strand, in the following colours: dark purple around the purple pansy; fuchsia inside the pink rose; black on all other back stitch marked on the key.

3 Decorate the fuchsia with French knots using two strands. Neatly finish the work and make up into a cushion, following the instructions for the Spring cushion on page 23.

Summer garland

If you're new to cross stitch, this charming garland design will suit even a novice stitcher. Whole cross stitch with back-stitch detail make up this elegant and simple design.

YOU WILL NEED

MATERIALS
fabric 28 hpi evenweave over
  two threads, 15 x 12 cm (6 x
  4 ½ in)
stranded cotton, as listed in key
needle
fabric-marker pen
scissors
wadding (batting)
crystal (glass) p

1 Work the cross stitch using two strands throughout.

2 Back stitch the detail, using one strand, in the following colours: grass green for stems on bottom half of design; dark rose pink for centres of pink flowers; sage green for stems on top half of chart; dark purple for detail on purple pansy and charcoal for detail on purple and yellow viola.

3 Neatly finish the design and mount in a crystal (glass) pot, following the instructions on page 17.

crystal (glass) pot

fabric

stranded cotton

wadding (batting)

fabric-marker pen

scissors

needle

key

•	pale mauve
◊	mid mauve
↑	deep mauve
↓	pale blush
✳	medium blush
⊓	very deep blush
⊐	bright green
⊞	pale sage green
◁	deep khaki
▶	pale pink
●	buttermilk

back stitch: grass green, dark rose pink, sage green, dark purple, charcoal

stitch count 51 x 41

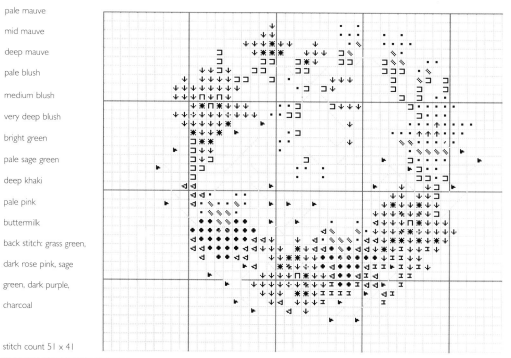

Butterfly gift tags

Flitting from bloom to bloom, the butterfly is a familiar sight during the summer months. Wrap a summer gift and add a delicate tag to give a personal touch.

YOU WILL NEED

MATERIALS
fabric: 18 hpi aida, 16 x 9 cm
  (6½ x 3½ in)
stranded cotton, as listed in key
needle
wadding (batting)
gift tags with apertures
  (openings)
scissors
glue

1 Work the cross stitch using two strands throughout.

2 Back stitch the detail, using one strand for each of the following colours: dark brown on the common butterfly and black on the blue butterfly.

3 Neatly finish the work, and place in a gift tag following the instructions for fitting into a greetings card on page 18.

gift tag

wadding (batting)

needle

stranded cotton

scissors

fabric-marker pen

fabric

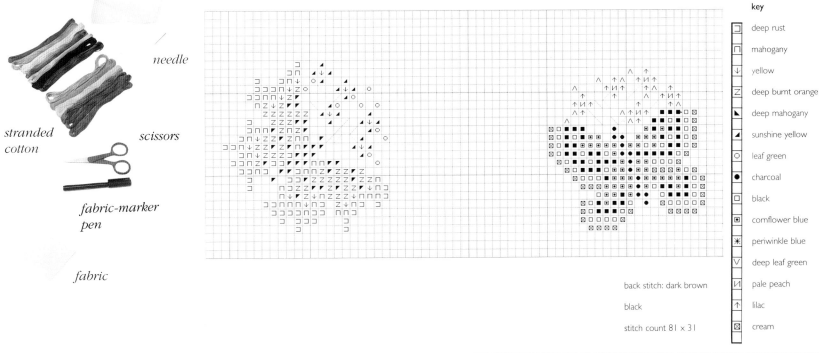

key

⊐	deep rust
⊓	mahogany
↓	yellow
Z	deep burnt orange
◤	deep mahogany
◢	sunshine yellow
○	leaf green
●	charcoal
□	black
⊡	cornflower blue
✳	periwinkle blue
∨	deep leaf green
И	pale peach
↑	lilac
⊠	cream

back stitch: dark brown

black

stitch count 81 x 31

Summer cottage

Tucked away at the end of a country lane, a summer cottage, with its abundant garden, makes a welcome oasis in the calm of the countryside. Bring it to life with this wonderful romantic cottage design.

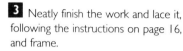

1 Work the cross stitch in two strands throughout.

2 Back stitch the detail marked on the chart using one strand of black.

3 Neatly finish the work and lace it, following the instructions on page 16, and frame.

YOU WILL NEED

MATERIALS
fabric: 30 hpi linen over two
   threads, 26 x 19 cm
   (10 x 7½ in)
stranded cotton, as listed in key
needle
mount board (backing board)
tape measure
fabric-marker pen
scissors
pins
threads
wadding (batting)
frame

fabric

stranded cotton

tape measure

scissors

fabric-marker pen

needle

wadding (batting)

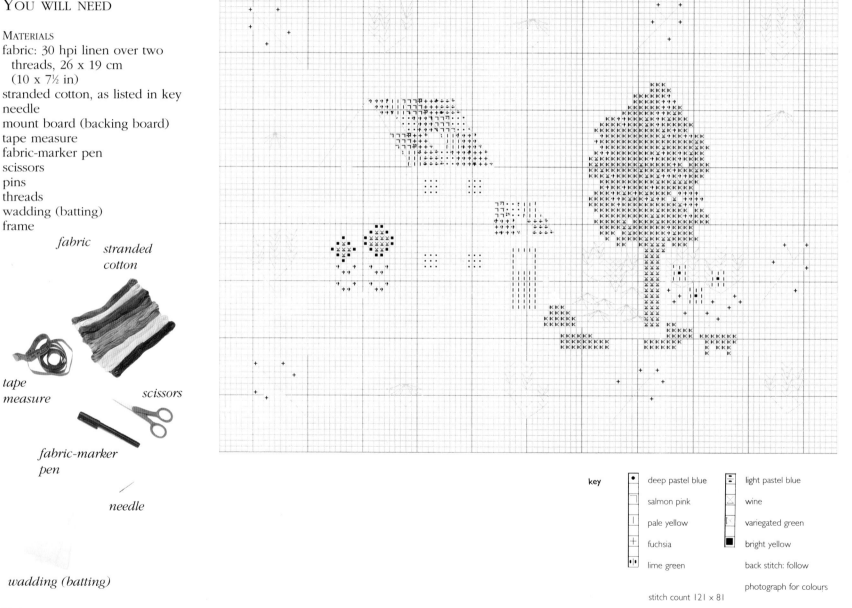

key

•	deep pastel blue	⊟	light pastel blue
⊓	salmon pink	⊠	wine
⌷	pale yellow	⋉	variegated green
+	fuchsia	■	bright yellow
⦙⦙	lime green		back stitch: follow photograph for colours

stitch count 121 x 81

Summer roses hat band

Add a touch of elegance to your summer hat by adding a decorative floral border. Repeat this single rose design and you'll be the belle of the garden party.

YOU WILL NEED

MATERIALS
fabric: 14hpi aida band,
   measure around the hat, plus
   3 cm (1¼ in)
stranded cotton, as listed in key
needles
pins
tape measure
scissors
thread
hat

hat

stranded cotton

scissors

tape measure

aida band

needles   *pins*

1 Work the cross stitch using two strands throughout.

2 Work the back stitch detail, using one strand, in the following colours: dark pink around the rose and dark green for the leaves.

key

·	light pink
⊙	mid pink
●	dark pink
×	dark green
✳	light green

back stitch: dark pink,

dark green

stitch count 61 × 31
(per repeat)

MAKING-UP INSTRUCTIONS

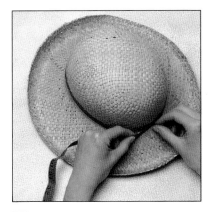

1 Measure the circumference of your hat and then divide the total measurement by two to get the centrepoint for the design. Using this measurement, mark the centre of the design on your band with a pin.

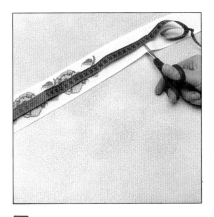

2 Work the design stitching your first repeat from the centrepoint. Continue repeating the flower design to fit around the rim of the hat. Using the centre point as a mid measurement, cut the band to length allowing 5 cm (2 in) at either end for finishing.

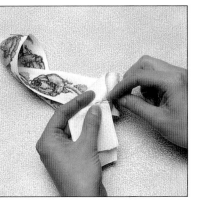

3 Place right sides together and stitch. Leave a 1.5 cm (½ in) seam allowance and press the seam flat. Turn the right way out and fit on to your hat with the seam at the back.

VARIATION
You can use any detail from the designs in this book to make pretty edgings for tablecloths, towels and napkins.

Summer sampler

Remind yourself of a perfect summer by stitching this crowded sampler full of everything special from the season. If you prefer, you could work the elements separately and mount them in a card.

YOU WILL NEED

MATERIALS
fabric 28 hpi evenweave over
    two threads, 27 x 31 cm (11 x
    12¼ in)
stranded cotton, as listed in key
needles
mount board (backing board)
tape measure
fabric-marker pen
scissors
wadding (batting)
pins
thread
frame

stranded cotton

scissors

tape measure   *fabric-marker pen*

wadding (batting)   *fabric*

thread

needle

key

•	medium pink
⧄	light pink
⫪	scarlet
=	medium purple
⎮	mauve
⫴	cerise
+	very dark brown
⊶	dark red brown
⋮	medium brown
⋈	light brown
⋉	black
⋊	blue
⁝⁝	yellow
○	orange
↓	dark green
←	medium green
⤢	light green
→	light brown
↑	dark brown/mid brown
■	red
●	light grey
⋀	white

back stitch: medium green,
dark grey, yellow, grey,
black, dark green, dark
brown, light green, light grey
light brown, very dark brown

stitch count 121 x 141

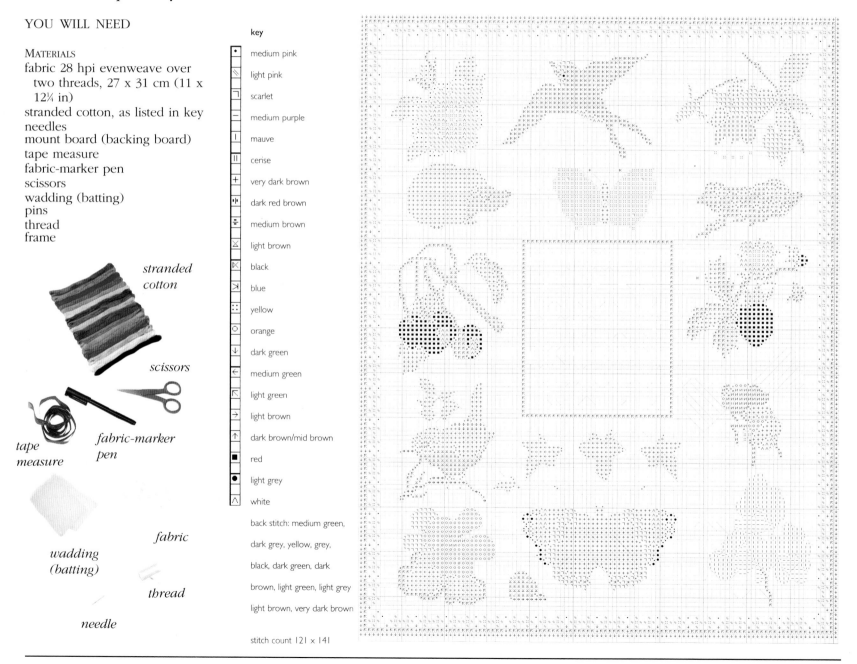

1 Work the cross stitch in two strands throughout.

2 Back stitch the following details marked on the chart, using one strand for each colour listed below. Dog rose: medium green for veins of leaves, dark grey for outlines and yellow for random French knots. Swallow: grey for wing details and black for outlines. Fuchsia: dark green for veins of leaves and dark grey for outlines. Hedgehog: dark grey for outlines and use two strands of long stitch randomly in dark brown for the spines. Brimstone butterfly: dark brown for body and feelers and dark grey for outlines. Frog: dark grey for outlines. Cherries: light green for veins on dark leaf and dark grey for outlines. Wren: dark green for veins on leaves and dark grey for outlines. Ivy: dark green for veins on leaves and dark grey for outlines. Bumble bee: light grey for wings, black for body and dark grey for outline of wings. Nasturtiums: black for internal lines, dark grey for outlines and two strands for French knot in centre of main flower. Snail: dark brown for whorl on inside of shell and dark grey for outline. Red admiral butterfly: light brown for internal lines on body and wings and very dark brown for outlines. Ladybird (ladybug): dark grey for outlines. Sweet peas: dark grey for outlines. Alphabet: two strands of dark green.

3 Neatly finish the work and lace it, following the instructions on page 16, and frame.

49

Summer house

In the middle of the garden sits the summer house, a glass retreat surrounded by flowers. It is a relaxing, peaceful haven where you can sit and watch the world go by.

YOU WILL NEED

MATERIALS
fabric: 14 hpi aida, 16 x 19 cm
  (61 x 71 in)
stranded cotton, as listed in key
needle
wadding (batting)
card with aperture (opening)
fabric-marker pen
scissors
glue

card

1 Work the cross stitch using two strands throughout.

2 Back stitch the detail on the chart, using one strand for each of the follow-ing colours: dark beige for the summer-house and mid forest green for the stems of flowers.

3 Neatly finish off the work and mount in a card following the instruc-tions on page 18.

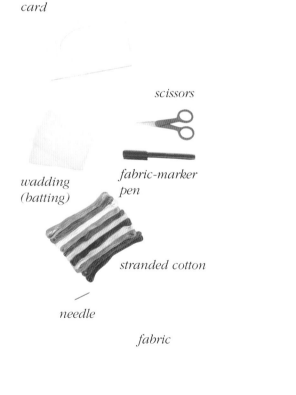

scissors

fabric-marker pen

wadding (batting)

stranded cotton

needle

fabric

key

○	mid purple
△	mid ochre
▲	dusky pink
⊞	light leaf green
↓	Christmas red
↑	bright yellow
∧	mid leaf green
И	mid mauve
‖	beige
⧉	deep ochre
✳	pearl grey

back stitch: dark beige,

mid forest green

stitch count 61 x 71

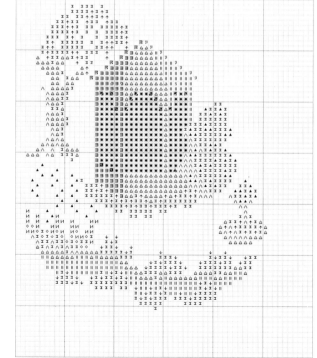

Collector's roses

A collector's cabinet provides ideal storage for your personal trinkets. Enhance it with this enchanting summer rose design for a truly superb display.

YOU WILL NEED

MATERIALS
fabric: 28 hpi evenweave over two threads, 15 x 15 cm (6 x 6 in)
stranded cotton, as listed in key
needles
yellow beads
piece of card (cardboard) about 15 cm (6 in) square
tape measure
scissors
wadding (batting)
glue
collector's cabinet

1 Work the cross stitch using two strands throughout.

2 Back stitch the detail on the chart, using one strand of black. Stitch yellow beads for the ends of the stamen and stitch French knots in black on the end of the butterfly's antennae.

3 Finish the work. Cut the card (cardboard) to the same size as the cabinet insert. Cut the wadding (batting) to the same size. Wrap the design over the card (cardboard) and wadding (batting), following the lacing instructions on page 16. Glue into the collector's cabinet.

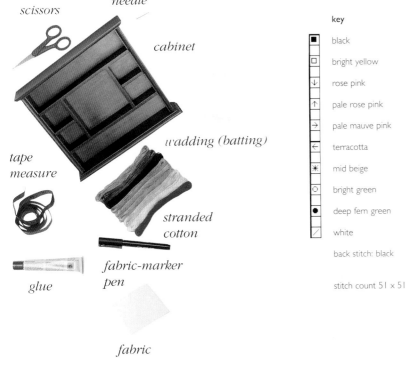

scissors
needle
cabinet
tape measure
wadding (batting)
stranded cotton
glue
fabric-marker pen
fabric

key

■	black
□	bright yellow
↓	rose pink
↑	pale rose pink
→	pale mauve pink
←	terracotta
✳	mid beige
○	bright green
●	deep fern green
	white

back stitch: black

stitch count 51 x 51

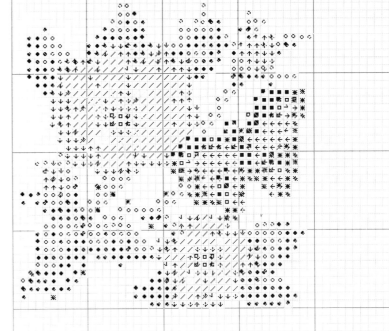

Country flowers scissors case

Keep your embroidery scissors safe inside this easy-to-make scissor case. Cornflowers and buttercups will make an heirloom case to keep the blades clean and sharp forever.

YOU WILL NEED

MATERIALS
fabric: 28 hpi evenweave over two threads, 12 x 15 cm (4¾ x 6 in)
stranded cotton, as listed in key
needles
pins
scissors
backing fabric, 12 x 15 cm (4¾ x 6 in)
lining fabric, 18 x 20 cm (6 x 8 in)
thread
lightweight iron-on interfacing

1 Work the cross stitch using two strands throughout.

2 Back stitch detail, using one strand for each of the following colours: very dark cornflower blue for harebells and cornflower; hunter green for stalks and leaves; dark mauve for bow and deep canary for cowslips and buttercups.

key

+ lilac

∧ pale yellow green

И pale yellow

╲ dusky pink

dark cornflower blue

↓ mid leaf green

Ǝ deep french navy

back stitch: very dark cornflower blue, hunter green, dark mauve, deep canary

stitch count 31 x 51

MAKING-UP INSTRUCTIONS

1 Cut two pairs of lining and fabric – triangular with the top edge 7.5 cm (3 in) and the length 10 cm (4 in), with 2 cm (¾ in) extra on all sides. Work the design centrally on one piece of fabric. Iron on interfacing to the back of all pieces. Pin one lining and backing piece right sides together and stitch along top edge, 1.5 cm (½ in) in. Do the same with remaining lining and front piece. Press both pieces flat with seams open.

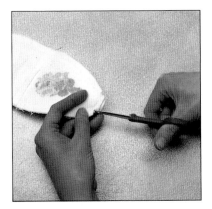

2 Pin the two pieces with right sides together and stitch around edge leaving approximately 4 cm (1½ in) gap at bottom of lining to allow for turning. Clip curves all along the edges.

3 Turn the work right side out and sew up the opening by hand with invisible stitches.

SEWING TIP

If you sew a piece of ribbon to either end of the scissor case, you can hang it around your neck and never lose your scissors again.

Lilac print

The lilac tree attracts the most beautiful butter-flies. From cabbage white to red admiral you'll be sure to find them hovering amongst the scented flowers of the lilac.

YOU WILL NEED

MATERIALS
fabric: 28 hpi evenweave over
two threads, 18 x 22 cm
(7 x 8½ in)
stranded cotton, as listed in key
needle
scissors
tape measure
fabric-marker pen
wadding (batting)

1 Work the cross stitch using two strands throughout.

2 Back stitch the detail on the charts, using one strand for each of the follow-ing colours: hunter green for the leaves; very dark mahogany for the butterflies and trunk and very light violet for the flowers.

3 Neatly finish the work. and lace it, following the instructions on page 16, and frame.

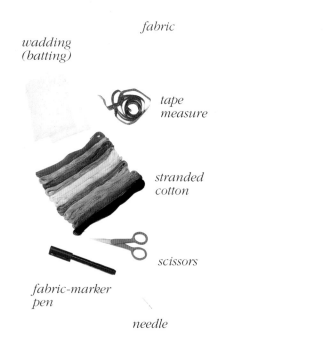

*wadding
(batting)*

fabric

*tape
measure*

*stranded
cotton*

scissors

*fabric-marker
pen*

needle

key

◁	black
►	coral red
○	bright yellow
●	mid sage green
↑	light sage green
↓	mid brown
→	deep lilac
□	lilac
‖	deep purple
=	brown

back stitch: hunter

green, very dark

mahogany, very

light violet

stitch count 71 x 91

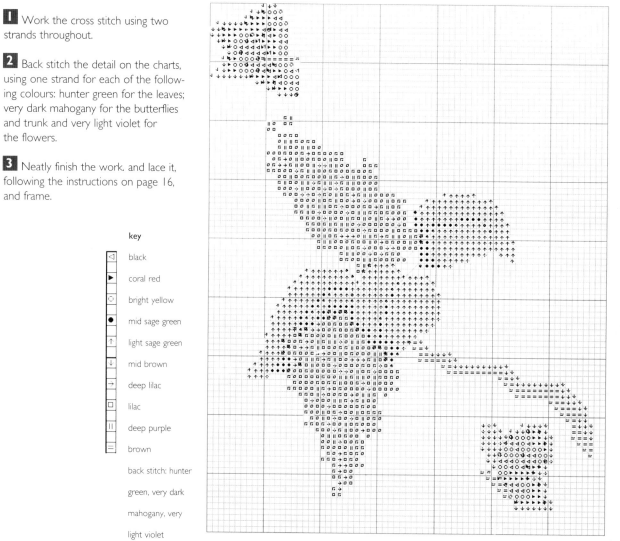

Lavender bag

Freshen up your wardrobe by hanging a sweet smelling lavender bag. The distinctive scent will remind you of long refreshing walks and summers past.

YOU WILL NEED

MATERIALS
fabric: 14 hpi aida, 15 x 16 cm
  (6 x 6 ½ in)
stranded cotton, as listed in key
needles
pins
scissors
tape measure
45.5 cm (18 in) lavender ribbon
  2.5 cm (1 in) wide
thread
dried lavender

1 Work the cross stitch in two strands throughout.

2 Back stitch the detail shown on the chart, using one strand of black.

key

✳	black
⊐	cream
I	deep green
●	sage green
○	pale sky blue
◁	pale periwinkle
▶	pearl grey

back stitch: black

stitch count 51 x 61

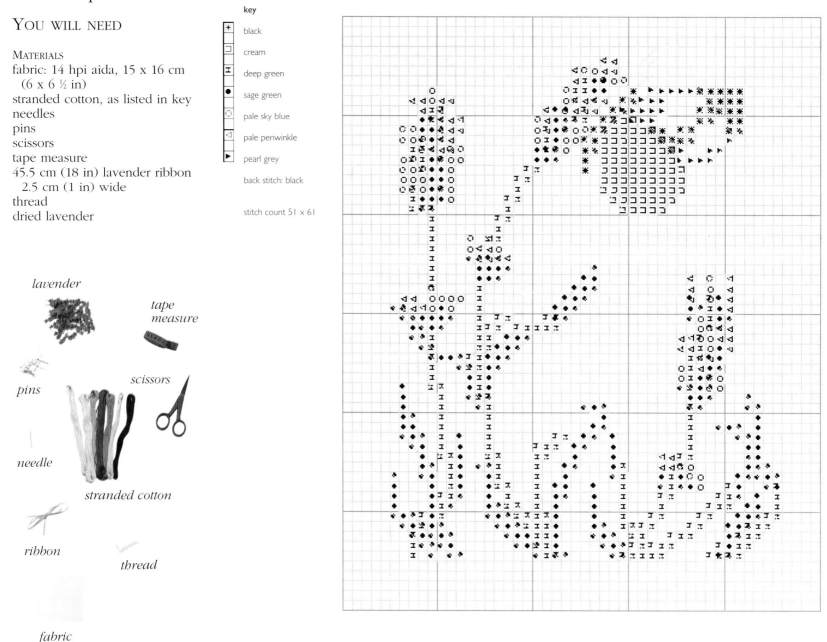

lavender

tape measure

pins

scissors

needle

stranded cotton

ribbon

thread

fabric

MAKING-UP INSTRUCTIONS

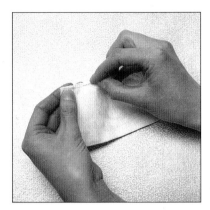

1 Fold under 1 cm (½ in) at the top of the work. Stitch to secure. With longer sides together, fold work in half, right sides enclosed, and stitch along this seam leaving a 1cm (½ in) edge.

2 Stitch a 1 cm (½ in) seam across the bottom of the bag. Turn to the right side and press. Taking a small pair of scissors, lightly snip vertically into the casing by the seam at the top of the bag at 1 cm (½ in) intervals. This is to form the ribbon casing.

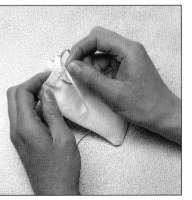

3 Thread the ribbon through the casing, using a large darning needle. Fill the bag with dried lavender and pull the ribbon to gather up the top. Tie in a bow to finish.

Strawberry weight

Lavish teas with fresh red strawberries epitomize all that is delicious about lazy, hazy, warm summer days. This strawberry paperweight keeps the memories fresh in your kitchen at all times.

YOU WILL NEED

MATERIALS
fabric: 14 hpi aida, 12.5 x
  12.5 cm (5 x 5 in)
stranded cotton, as listed in key
needle
scissors
fabric-marker pen
paperweight
glue

1 Work the cross stitch using three strands throughout.

2 Back stitch the detail on the chart, using one strand for each of the following colours: deep garnet around the strawberries; dark green around the leaves and on stalks.

3 Use one strand of very light beige brown, wrapped 2–3 times around the needle, for random French knots on the strawberries for seeds.

4 Neatly finish off the work. Cut to size and place in the paperweight, gluing it to the piece of card (cardboard) provided with the paperweight.

paperweight

glue

scissors

fabric-marker pen

fabric

needle

stranded cotton

key

⊙	deep garnet
●	garnet
■	cream
⊐	mid grass green
□	mid leaf green

back stitch: deep garnet, dark green, very light beige

stitch count 41 x 41

Autumn leaves pot stand

With its large leaves and fruit, the horse chestnut makes a distinctive seasonal image. Ir an arrangement with oak leaves and acorns, it makes a perfect design for this pot stand.

YOU WILL NEED

MATERIALS
fabric 28 hpi evenweave over
   two threads, 14.5 x 14.5cm
   (6 x 6 in)
stranded cotton, as listed in key
needle
tape measure
fabric-marker pen
scissors
pot stand

1 Work the cross stitch in two strands throughout.

2 Back stitch the detail, using one strand for each of the following colours: very dark avocado green for oak leaves and dark mocha brown for remainder.

3 Neatly finish off the work. Cut to the same size as the aperture (opening) and place inside the pot stand. Secure with the backing card (cardboard) provided with the stand.

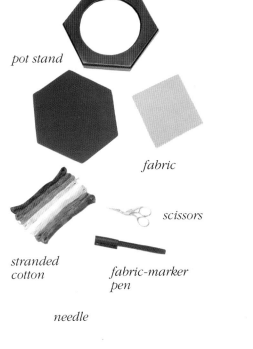

pot stand

fabric

stranded cotton

fabric-marker pen

scissors

needle

key

◥	deep mustard
‖	mustard
+	mahogany
⊕	pale mahogany
⊟	cream
∧	mid sienna
⋈	pale sienna
◇	mid beige
∷	olive green
▶	deep beige green

back stitch: very dark
avocado green, very
dark mocha brown

stitch count 51 x 51

Autumn cushion

With the russets and browns of autumn beginning to appear, the colourful and distinctive blooms of this delightful cushion will provide a perfect memento of this time of year.

1 Work the cross stitch in two strands throughout.

2 Back stitch the details, in one strand, in the following colours: dark forest green for the internal detail on leaves (bottom centre and left); medium forest green for external detail on leaves (bottom left and centre); salmon on stems (bottom left); dark forest green for leaf detail (top right); dark pink for detail on flowers (bottom left); brown for leaf detail across the top.

3 Use one strand of light yellow wrapped around the needle 2–3 times, for French knots in the centres of the purple flowers.

YOU WILL NEED

MATERIALS
fabric: 14 hpi aida, 33 x 33 cm
  (13 x 13 in)
stranded cotton, as listed in key
needle
thimble
pins
scissors
tape measure
fabric-marker pen
thread
fabric for cushion
cushion pad

fabric

scissors

fabric-marker pen

needle

tape measure

stranded cotton

thimble

pins

4 Neatly finish off the work and make up into your cushion following the instructions for the Spring cushion on page 23.

key

⊓	steel grey
−	pale yellow
I	medium mint green
+	light mint green
⊠	grass green
⊠	dark grass green
∧	pale pink
И	rose pink
◿	deep rose pink
╱	medium rose pink
⊠	olive green
○	light olive green
T	mid cream
⊥	deep cream
☰	muddy gold
◁	apricot
▶	gold
⊟	dull orange
⊓	mid yellow green
✶	dark yellow green
▲	yellow green
●	cream
■	red orange
↑	deep red
→	dark gold
⌐	rust
△	mauve
←	deep mauve

back stitch: dark forest green,

medium forest green, salmon pink, dark forest

green, dark pink, brown, light yellow

stitch count 151 x 151

Nesting squirrel pot

Saving his store of nuts for the winter, the squirrel hoards and stockpiles. This useful pot design celebrates his perennial task. Why not stitch it for a friend so they can hoard their trinkets inside?

YOU WILL NEED

MATERIALS
fabric: 18 hpi aida, 12.5 x 11 cm
  (5 x 4 ½ in)
stranded cotton, as listed in key
needle
scissors
fabric-marker pen
wadding (batting)
round pot

1 Cross stitch all four leaves using one strand, and two strands for the rest of the design.

2 Back stitch the detail using one strand of very dark mahogany throughout.

3 Neatly finish the work. Mount in a round pot following the instructions on page 17.

round pot *fabric*

wadding (batting) *needle*

stranded cotton

scissors

fabric-marker pen

key

✳	dark khaki green
○	mid mahogany
●	light khaki green
↑	very dark coral red
↓	very light brown
←	light tan
→	light mahogany
◁	white
►	dark beige brown
⊓	black
⊐	pearl grey
⊓	light beige brown

back stitch: very dark mahogany

stitch count 51 x 41

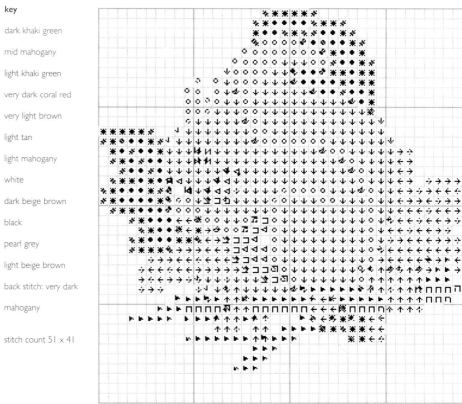

Halloween pumpkin

Fields of pumpkins, and boughs full of red and green apples symbolize this wonderful time of year, and make a perfect design for a special Halloween card.

YOU WILL NEED

MATERIALS
fabric: 28 hpi evenweave over
two threads, 14.5 x 12.5 cm
   (5½ x 5 in)
stranded cotton, as listed in key
needle
fabric-marker pen
scissors
wadding (batting)
card with aperture (opening)
glue

1 Work the cross stitch in two strands throughout.

2 Back stitch the detail, using one strand for each of the following colours: black around the eye; brown around the mouse and whiskers; green around apple and leaf veins; yellow for highlights on apple, and dark gold brown around the stalk and on the pumpkin.

3 Neatly finish off the design and mount in the card following the instructions on page 18.

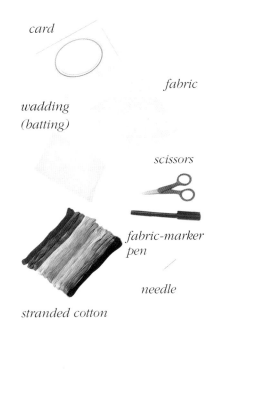

card

fabric

*wadding
(batting)*

scissors

*fabric-marker
pen*

needle

stranded cotton

key

✱	pink
•	black
I	light grey brown
+	dark grey brown
⊠	red
⋉	light green
∧	brown
И	dark gold
⋊	light gold
∷	dark gold brown
●	dark green

back stitch: black,

brown, green, yellow.

dark gold brown

stitch count 51 x 41

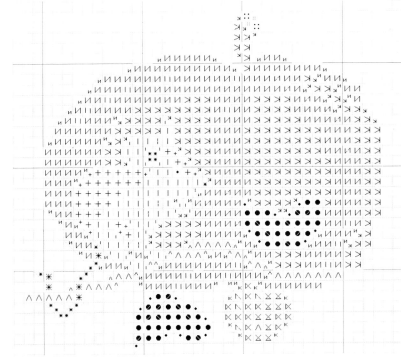

Harvest mouse

With fields of fresh wheat ready for harvest, the field mouse is a common sight on farms during the autumn months. Why not try this waste canvas project to enhance a T-shirt or baseball cap for a child?

YOU WILL NEED

MATERIALS
fabric: 14 hpi waste canvas,
  11 x 12.5 cm (4 x 5 in)
stranded cotton, as listed in key
needles
scissors
cloth or sponge
water
tweezers
cotton T-shirt

T-shirt

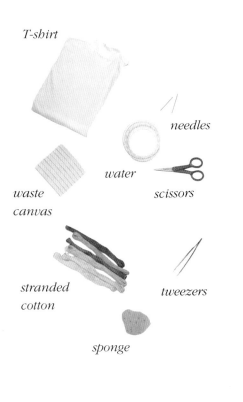

waste canvas

needles

water

scissors

stranded cotton

tweezers

sponge

1 Work the cross stitch using two strands of stranded cotton throughout.

2 Back stitch the detail, using one strand, in the following colours: mid rose for the paws; black for the eye; dark mahogany for the rest of the mouse and dark flesh for the corn.

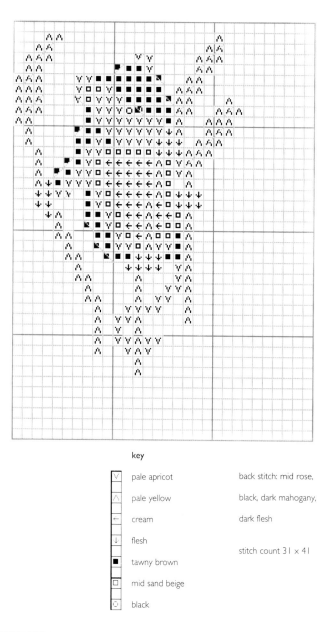

key

symbol	colour		back stitch
V	pale apricot		back stitch: mid rose,
∧	pale yellow		black, dark mahogany,
←	cream		dark flesh
↓	flesh		
■	tawny brown		stitch count 31 x 41
□	mid sand beige		
◌	black		

WORKING WASTE CANVAS

1 Tack (baste) the waste canvas to your garment where you want the design to be, and work your design.

2 Since the grid lines of the waste canvas are only a guide to positioning your stitches, extra care needs to be taken to keep your stitching even. The following hints might help:
a) Insert your needle in the centre of the waste canvas grid holes.
b) Make sure your stitches come up and go down in the same spot in the holes each time on your base material.
c) Start and finish off your threads very securely.
d) Do not stitch through the threads of the waste canvas – take particular care with fractional stitches.

3 When all the stitching is complete, remove tacking (basting) and trim away excess waste canvas. Take a clean wet cloth or sponge and dampen your work thoroughly.

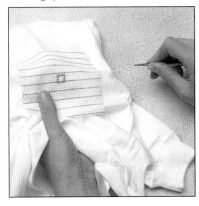

4 Use tweezers to pull out each thread of waste canvas individually. If you have any difficulty at this stage, either you have not dissolved all the starch holding the waste canvas together or you have stitched through the canvas threads. In the former case, re-dampen your work and try again with the tweezers. If you have stitched through the waste canvas, you will need to cut the canvas either side of the trapped thread – be careful not to cut any of the cross stitching.

Autumn cottage

Falling leaves and brisk, fresh winds tell us that autumn is here. This picturesque little cottage weathers the elements as it stands guard and experiences the changing climate.

YOU WILL NEED

MATERIALS
fabric: 30 hpi linen over two
  threads, 26 x 20 cm
  (10½ x 8 in)
stranded cotton, as listed in key
needle
scissors
fabric-marker pen
tape measure
wadding (batting)
mount board (backing board)
pins
thread frame

fabric

stranded cotton

scissors

*tape
measure*

*fabric-marker
pen*

needle

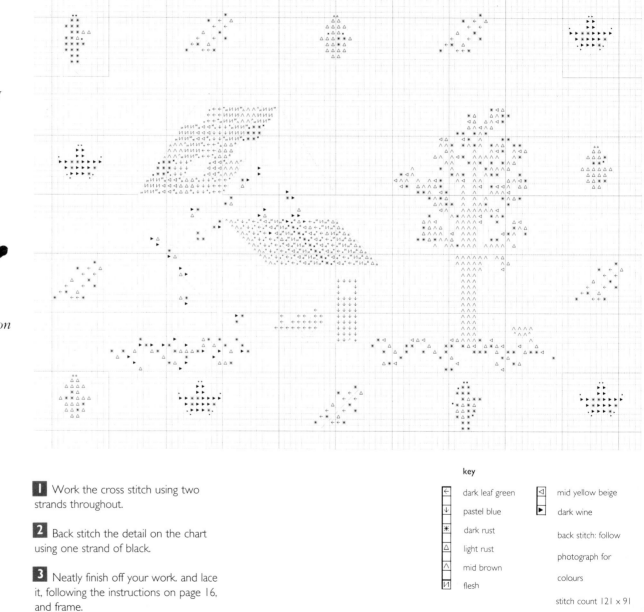

1 Work the cross stitch using two strands throughout.

2 Back stitch the detail on the chart using one strand of black.

3 Neatly finish off your work. and lace it, following the instructions on page 16, and frame.

key

←	dark leaf green	◁	mid yellow beige
↓	pastel blue	▶	dark wine
＊	dark rust		back stitch: follow
△	light rust		photograph for
∧	mid brown		colours
И	flesh		

stitch count 121 x 91

Blackberry card

Do you remember autumn afternoons spent collecting delicious blackberries to make jelly? Stitch this card in memory of those nostalgic times.

YOU WILL NEED

MATERIALS
fabric: 18 hpi aida, 12.5 x 11 cm
  (5 x 4½ in)
stranded cotton, as listed in key
needle
scissors
fabric-marker pen
wadding (batting)
card with aperture (opening)
glue

1 Work the blackberries and flowers using two strands of cross stitch. Use one strand for cross stitching the leaves.

2 Back stitch the detail, using one strand, in the following colours: very dark dusty rose for the flowers; dark antique violet for unripe blackberries; black for ripe blackberries and hunter green for the leaves.

3 Neatly finish off the work and mount in a greetings card, following the instructions on page 18.

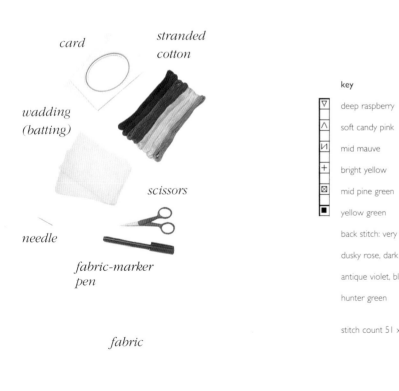

card

stranded cotton

wadding (batting)

scissors

needle

fabric-marker pen

fabric

key

▽	deep raspberry
∧	soft candy pink
И	mid mauve
+	bright yellow
⊠	mid pine green
■	yellow green

back stitch: very dark dusky rose, dark antique violet, black, hunter green

stitch count 51 x 41

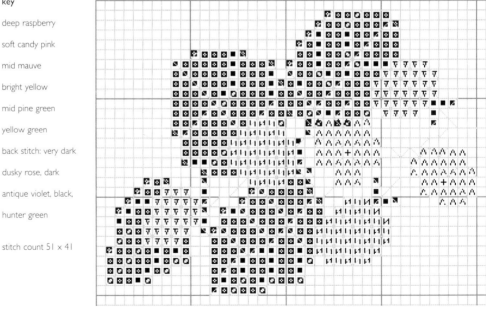

Apple and pears placemats

Cross stitch is so versatile, you can use it for almost anything. Creating a complete place setting can be satisfying, practical and extremely attractive – use the same chart for each, picking out either the pear or the apple for the napkin holder.

YOU WILL NEED

MATERIALS
fabric: ivory 11 hpi aida
  35.5 x 30.5 cm (14 x 12 in)
ivory 11 hpi waste canvas
  approx 12.5 x 12.5 cm (5 x 5 in)
ivory 18 hpi aida approx
  7.5 x 7.5 cm (3 x 3 in)
stranded cotton, as listed in key
needles
thimble
scissors
fabric-marker pen
pins
tape measure
iron-on interfacing
cream cotton backing fabric
napkin
napkin holder

fabrics

napkin

napkin holder

fabric-marker pen

stranded cotton

thimble

tape measure

needle

scissors

FOR THE PLACEMAT

1 Position the design 4 cm (1½ in) up from the bottom edge of the fabric and 4 cm (1½ in) in from the left-hand edge. Use three strands throughout for the cross stitch.

2 Turn under the edges by 1.5 cm (½ in) all around, and iron flat. Take a piece of medium weight iron-on interfacing 33 x 30 cm (13 x 11 in) and iron on the reverse of the design, placing it between the turned edges

3 Take a piece of cream-coloured cotton backing fabric 35.5 x 30.5 cm (14 x 12 in), turn under a 1.5 cm (½ in) edge all around and press. Place on reverse of placemat with the turned edges sandwiched together, pin and slip stitch the backing to the placemat.

FOR THE NAPKIN

1 Tack (baste) the waste canvas to a corner of the napkin and stitch the design, using 3 strands throughout. Dampen and remove the waste canvas and tacking (basting) stitches.

FOR THE NAPKIN HOLDER

1 Stitch either the pear or the apple using one strand throughout. Trim aida to approx 5 x 5 cm (2 x 2 in) and iron under edges all round to make the finished piece approximately 4 x 4 cm (1½ x 1½ in) to fit napkin holder. Insert into holder.

key

✳	mid pistachio green
•	dark pistachio green
⋈	light yellow beige
○	light pistachio green
▼	mid golden olive
◁	mid yellow beige
►	mid avocado green
И	very light avocado green
■	light avocado green
∧	coral
⊐	dark coral
⊓	very dark beige grey
▽	very dark pistachio green
◇	deep beige grey

stitch count 41 x 51

69

Chicken tea cosy

Outside the farmhouse door the yard is full
of pecking hens, ducks and geese. Amid the
cackling din, the farmer's wife goes about her
daily chores. It's a lively scene with an air of
gentle tranquillity. And a challenging project for
even the most experienced stitcher.

YOU WILL NEED

MATERIALS
fabric: 14 hpi aida, 42 x 32 cm
  (16½ x 12½ in)
stranded cotton, as listed in key
needle
scissors
pins
fabric for cosy
fabric-marker pen
thread
tape measure
wadding (batting)

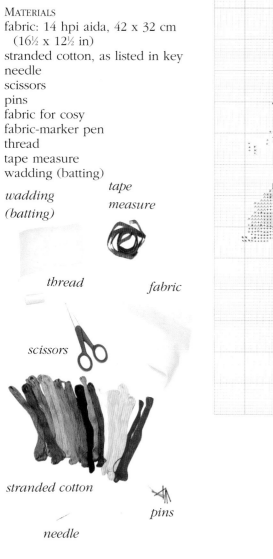

*wadding
(batting)*

*tape
measure*

thread

fabric

scissors

stranded cotton

pins

needle

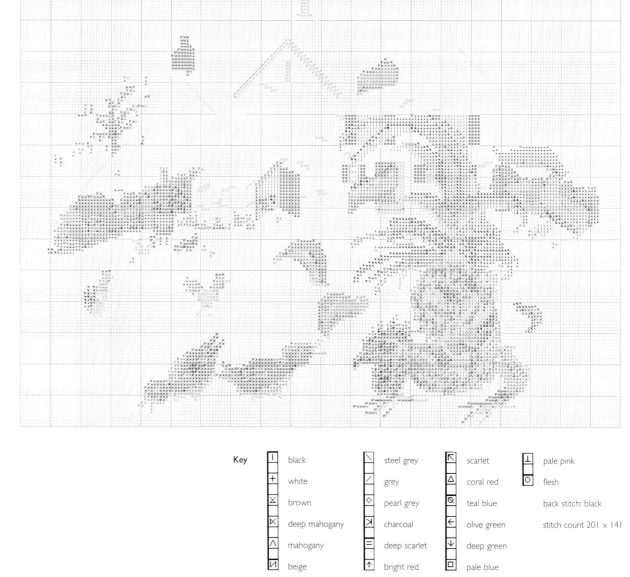

Key

Symbol	Colour	Symbol	Colour	Symbol	Colour	Symbol	Colour
I	black	\	steel grey	↖	scarlet	⊥	pale pink
+	white	/	grey	△	coral red	⊙	flesh
⊠	brown	◇	pearl grey	⊠	teal blue		back stitch: black
⊠	deep mahogany	⊠	charcoal	←	olive green		stitch count 201 x 141
∧	mahogany	=	deep scarlet	↓	deep green		
⋈	beige	↑	bright red	☐	pale blue		

MAKING-UP INSTRUCTIONS

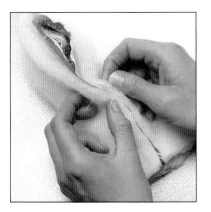

1 Work the cross stitch using two strands throughout. Back stitch the detail using one strand of black. Cut the design and backing fabric into a semi-circle, with the bottom of the design along the straight edge. Sew the design to the backing fabric with right sides together, leaving a 1.5 cm (½ in) seam.

2 Sew the lining together, along the semi-circle, leaving the bottom edge open. Attach the wadding (batting) by tacking (basting) the seam to the wrong side of the front and back of the cosy.

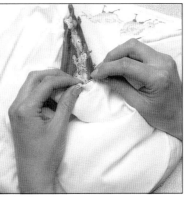

3 Attach the cosy to the lining, right sides together, leaving a gap of 1.5 cm (½ in) for turning.

4 Turn the cosy right sides out, and finish off the open edge with small invisible stitches.

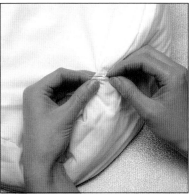

Bees and honey tea towel

Add a little decorative detail to your kitchen linen to grace your towel rail, by stitching this original yet simple hive design.

YOU WILL NEED

MATERIALS
fabric: aida 14 hpi tea towel
stranded cotton, as listed in key
needle
scissors

tea towel

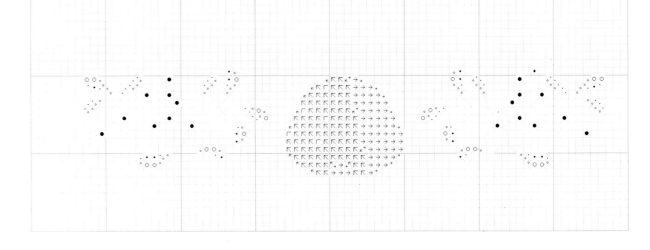

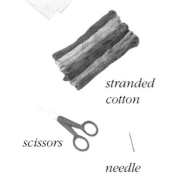

stranded cotton

scissors

needle

1 Work the cross stitch using two strands throughout. Back stitch detail in the following colours: dark green for the leaf detail (two strands); dark pink for the flowers and brown for the hive (two strands).

2 To stitch the work evenly on the tea towel, start at the centre and stitch a hive with floral detail on either side.

3 Leave 4 holes before working your next repeat. Make sure you balance the design by working the same element on both the left and right sides of the centre.

key

·	medium green
○	light green
●	pink
↖	golden brown
→	dark golden brown

back stitch: dark green,

dark pink, brown

stitch count 81 × 31
(per repeat)

Autumn sampler

With animals scurrying for shelter and preparing for the onslaught of winter, the autumn is a busy time in the country. This lovely sampler is packed with country plants and creatures which can be seen regularly during this time of year.

YOU WILL NEED

MATERIALS
fabric: 28 hpi evenweave over
  two threads, 27 x 31 cm 10½ x
  12 in)
stranded cotton, as listed in key
needle
scissors
fabric-marker pen
tape measure
wadding (batting)
pins
thread
frame

stranded cotton

scissors

tape measure

fabric-marker pen

wadding (batting)

needle

fabric

key

•	medium green
⅂	light green
—	red
I	scarlet
II	blue
+	black
⹀	white
⌂	yellow
⋉	light grey
∧	dark grey
Ͷ	black
▶	light pink/very light green
◁	red/very light green
▲	mid grey/mid brown
■	medium grey
⬉	mauve
←	dark purple
↓	rust brown
⊥	very dark brown
○	dark brown
⠿	medium brown
⊠	light brown
◇	cream
▽	very light green

For back stitch colours,

see step two on page 75.

stitch count 121 × 141

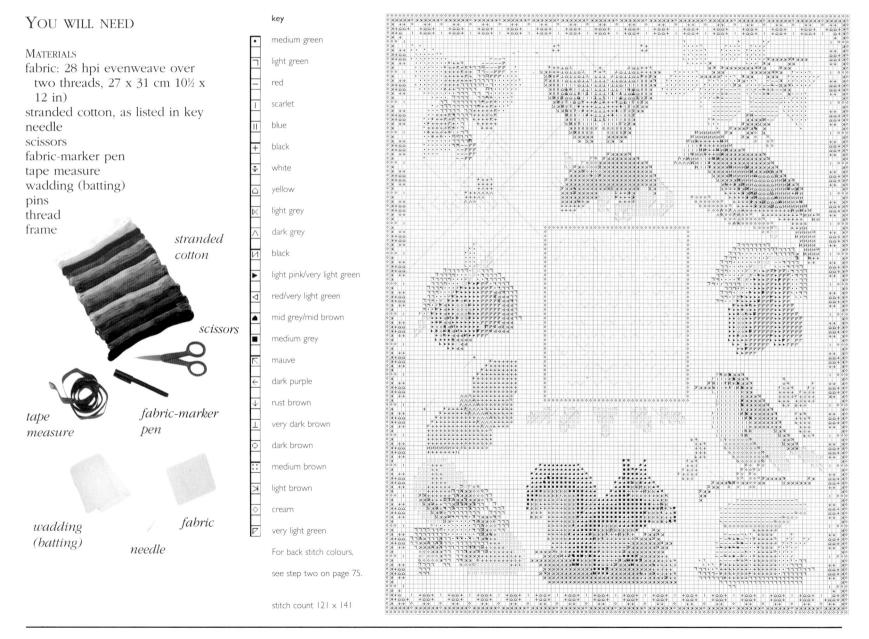

1 Work the cross stitch using two stands throughout.

2 Back stitch the details, using one strand, for each of the following colours. Blackberries: dark green for veins on leaves; dark purple for outline of blackberries; mauve for markings on berries; dark grey for outlining else-where. Tortoiseshell butterfly: black for internal markings and dark brown for outlines. Rosehips: dark green for veins on leaves; dark grey for outlines. Spider and spider's web: black for spider's legs and outline; pearly white thread for spider's web. Harvest mouse: dark grey for whiskers and outlines. Goldfinch: dark grey for outline. Crab apples: medium brown for bud marks on bottom of apples; dark grey for outline and dark green for veins on leaves. Pears: medium brown for bud marks, dark grey for outlines. Large white but-terfly: dark grey for veins on lower wings; and dark grey for outlines. Oak leaves: dark brown for veins on leaves; dark grey for outlines. Robin: dark brown for veins on leaves and markings on wings; dark grey for outlines. Hazelnuts: very dark brown for veins on leaves; dark grey for outlines. Squirrel: dark grey for outline; white French knot for squirrel's eye and sew long stitches at random lengths follow-ing the shape of the tail. Funghi: white French knots at random and dark grey for outlines. Alphabet letters: use two strands of dark brown and also for outline of box.

3 Neatly finish off the work and lace it, following the instructions on page 16, and frame.

Holly bookmark

Deck the halls with holly or simply stitch some to create a border for this nostalgic winter scene. This design will make a super present for a book lover.

YOU WILL NEED

MATERIALS
fabric: 18 hpi aida bookmark,
  8 x 18 cm (3 x 7 in)
stranded cotton, as listed in key
needle
scissors
felt

bookmark

stranded cotton

scissors

needle

felt

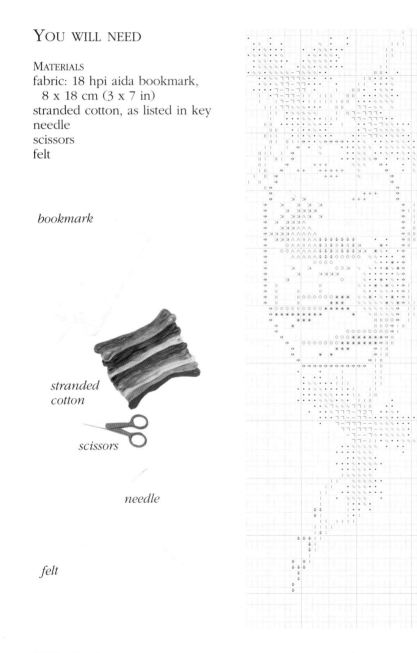

key

•	mid green
⟍	dark green
⌐	red
=	orange
I	light brown
II	dark brown
+	light blue
⊹	gold
⊟	light gold
∧	very light fawn
○	grey
⊠	light blue grey
✳	beige

back stitch: red, dark brown, light blue grey

stitch count 41 x131

1 Work the cross stitch using two strands throughout.

2 Back stitch the detail, using one strand for each of the following colours: red for detail on Christmas tree; dark brown for fence and house detail and light blue grey for smoke coming out of the chimney.

3 Neatly finish the work and finish into a bookmark, following the instructions on page 19.

Cottage snow scene card

A typical sight during the winter is the robin red-breast proudly singing his vibrant song. Perched on a branch, he cuts an imposing figure in the countryside.

YOU WILL NEED

MATERIALS
fabric: 18 hpi aida, 17 x 17 cm
  7 x 7 in)
stranded cotton, as listed in key
needle
scissors
fabric-marker pen
wadding (batting)
card with aperture (opening)

1 Work the cross stitch using two strands throughout.

2 Back stitch the detail on the chart using one strand in black.

3 Neatly finish your work and mount in a card, following the instructions on page 18.

card

scissors

stranded cotton

fabric-marker pen

fabric

wadding (batting)

needle

key

I	black
+	white
⋈	light brown
∧	mid brown
И	salmon pink
＼	pale salmon pink
/	blue grey
◇	pearl grey
⋊	deep green
○	deep olive green
⊥	yellow green

back stitch: black

stitch count 91 x 81

Garden fairy

Perched in a prime position on your tree the
garden fairy will bring a touch of country magic to
your Christmas!

YOU WILL NEED

MATERIALS
fabric: 14 hpi plastic canvas,
    18 x 20 cm (7 x 8 in)
stranded cotton, as listed in key
gold thread
needles
scissors
green felt 18 x 20 cm (7 x 8 in)

*plastic
canvas*

*gold
thread*

felt

scissors

needle

*stranded
cotton*

key

‖	white
=	deep red
⠿	beige
○	pale yellow
●	sunshine yellow
✳	cream
◁	pale sage green
▶	mid sage green
↑	flesh
↓	mid blush

back stitch: very dark

blue green, very dark

coral red, dark flesh,

muddy gold (for

veins on wings)

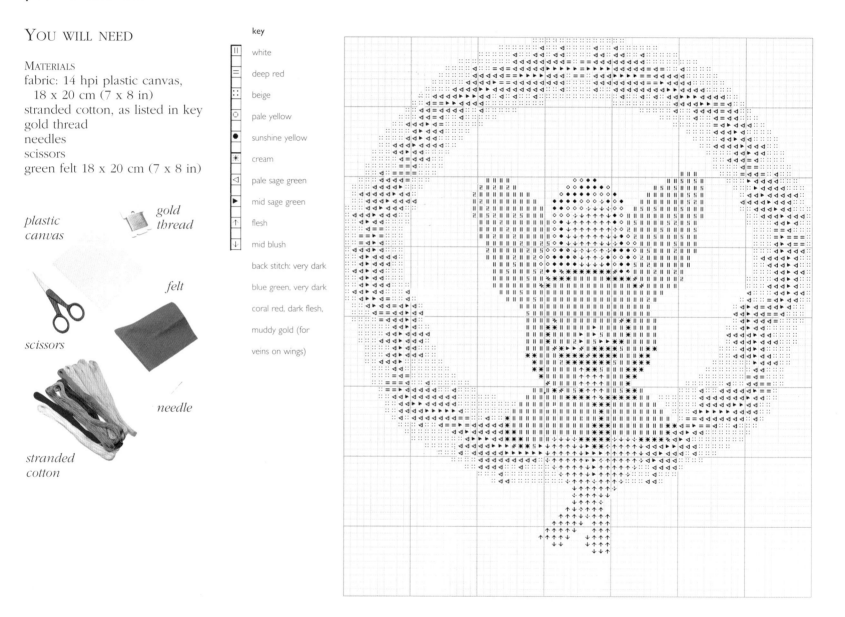

MAKING-UP INSTRUCTIONS

1 Work the cross stitch onto the plastic canvas using three strands throughout. Back stitch the detail, using one strand, in the following colours: very dark blue green for holly wreath; very dark coral red for mouth; dark flesh for fairy. Use two strands of muddy gold for back stitching on the wings. Stitch one French knot in dark flesh for each fairy eye.

2 Carefully cut away the canvas around the edge of your design, taking care not to snip the stitches.

3 Oversew (slip stitch) the edges to cover all the raw canvas using two strands of very dark blue green.

4 Cut off any knobbly corners for a neat finish and attach the felt. You can either use sticky-backed felt or sew on ordinary felt using small invisible stitches.

Mistletoe gift tag

When you give your Christmas presents surprise the recipients with dainty, hand-stitched tags.

YOU WILL NEED

MATERIALS
fabric: 18 hpi aida, 9 x 8 cm
  (3¾ x 3¼ in)
stranded cotton, as listed in key
needle
scissors
wadding (batting)
gift tag with aperture (opening)
fabric-marker pen
glue

1 Work the cross stitch using one strand throughout.

2 Back stitch the detail, using one strand, in the following colours: mid olive green for the left leaf and deep olive green for the right leaf.

3 Neatly finish off the work and mount within a gift tag, following the instructions for mounting a card on page 18.

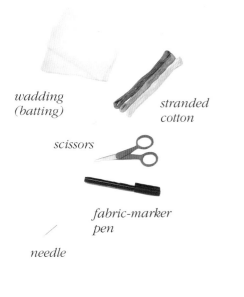

fabric

gift tag

wadding (batting)

stranded cotton

scissors

fabric-marker pen

needle

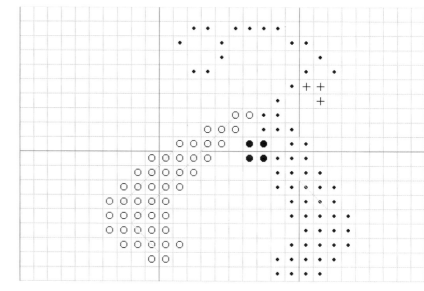

key

•	deep olive green
○	mid olive green
●	cream
+	pearl

back stitch: mid olive green, deep olive green

stitch count 31 x 21

Cyclamen card

This is not much evidence of flowers during the winter months, yet in households across the land the cyclamen blooms eternal.

YOU WILL NEED

MATERIALS
fabric: 18 hpi aida, 10 x 12.5 cm
  (4 x 5 in)
stranded cotton, as listed in key
needle
scissors
fabric-marker pen
wadding (batting)
card with aperture (opening)
glue

1 Work the cross stitch using two strands throughout.

2 Back stitch the detail, using one strand, for each of the following colours: dark cranberry around the flowers and dark blue green around the leaves and stems.

3 Neatly finish your work and mount in a card, following the instructions on page 18.

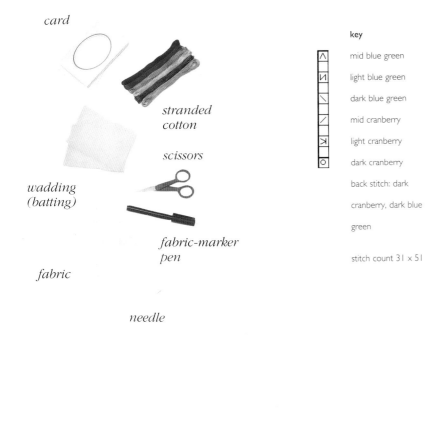

card

stranded cotton

scissors

wadding (batting)

fabric-marker pen

fabric

needle

key

∧	mid blue green
и	light blue green
⌐	dark blue green
∕	mid cranberry
и	light cranberry
○	dark cranberry

back stitch: dark cranberry, dark blue green

stitch count 31 x 51

Winter cushion

With holly, mistletoe and Christmas roses, this
elegant cushion will make an elegant centrepiece
for your festive display.

YOU WILL NEED

MATERIALS
fabric: 14 hpi navy blue aida,
   36 x 36 cm (14 x 14 in)
stranded cotton, as listed in key
needles
scissors
thimble
pins
fabric-marker pen
tape measure
contrasting fabric for cushion
thread
cushion pad

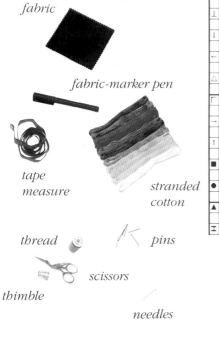

fabric

fabric-marker pen

tape measure

stranded cotton

thread   *pins*

thimble

scissors

needles

key

I	white
+	mint green
ᵘ	very pale pine green
K	bright yellow
Λ	bright green
II	pale yellow
	deep red
	Christmas red
⊠	light leaf green
≡	deep leaf green
☐	mid leaf green
⊥	very pale yellow
ι	light mocha
←	deep mocha
△	mid beige
Γ	orange brown
⊣	deep pine green
↑	mid pine green
■	light pine green
●	red
▲	pale pink
⊥	sunshine yellow

back stitch: slate green,
white, dark brown,
Christmas red, deep olive
green, olive green, pale
yellow, bright yellow

stitch count 151 x 151

1 Work the cross stitch using two strands throughout.

2 Back stitch the detail, using one strand, for each of the following colours: slate green for lines dividing the Christmas rose petals; white for outside edges of Christmas roses; dark brown dividing poinsettia petals; Christmas red for outside edges of poinsettia flowers; deep olive green for outlines of poinsettia flowers; olive green for poinsettia and holly. Use two strands for long stitch in pale yellow for stamens of Christmas rose, and two strands for French knots: pale yellow at the end of each Christmas rose stamen and bright yellow randomly to fill centre of poinsettia flowers.

3 Finish off the work and make into a cushion, following the instructions for the Spring cushion on page 23.

Poinsettia ornaments

Brighten up your Christmas tree with these imaginative, easy-to-stitch ornaments.

YOU WILL NEED

MATERIALS
fabric: 18 hpi aida, 12.5 x
  12.5 cm (5 x 5 in)
stranded cotton, as listed in key
needle
scissors
fabric-marker pen
thread
polystyrene ball
glue
gold braid
ribbon

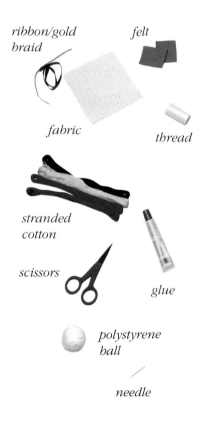

ribbon/gold braid

felt

fabric

thread

stranded cotton

scissors

glue

polystyrene ball

needle

MAKING-UP INSTRUCTIONS

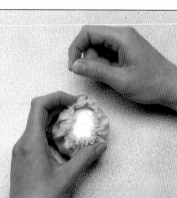

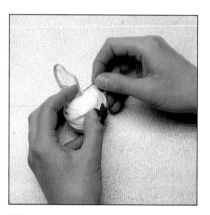

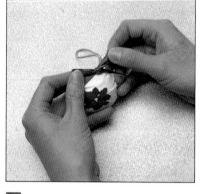

1 Work the cross stitch using two strands throughout. Back stitch around the outline, using one strand in black. Once the design has been worked, cut a circle from the fabric with the design in the centre. Run a gathering thread around the edge of the circle and pull it up around the polystyrene ball.

2 Attach a loop of braid to the top of the ball to make a hanging hook.

3 Tie a bow from ribbon at the base of the braid.

4 Finish with a small circle of felt to cover the gathering at the back.

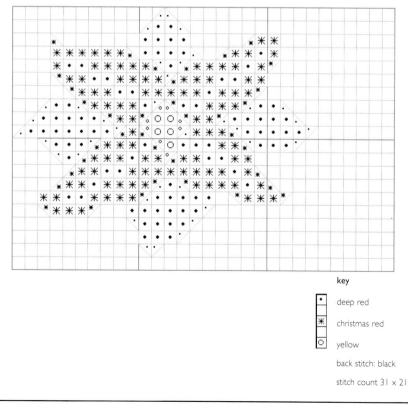

key

•	deep red
✳	christmas red
○	yellow

back stitch: black

stitch count 31 x 21

Advent calendar

With only 24 days to Christmas Eve, you can mark each one by stitching this elegant advent calendar, complete with brass rings, on which you can hang candies to note each day of the countdown.

YOU WILL NEED

MATERIALS

fabric: 28 hpi evenweave over
   two threads, 24 x 26 cm (9½ x
   10¼ in)
stranded cotton, as listed in key
needles
scissors
thimble
pins
fabric-marker pen
tape measure
wadding (batting)
mount board (backing board)
frame
24 small brass curtain rings
5m (180 in) reel of 0 .5 cm
   (¼ in) green silk ribbon
24 wrapped candies

key

	white
	hunter green
	light lemon
	dark lemon
	cream
	mid pine green
	light pine green

back stitch: dark
lemon, hunter green,
very dark flesh

stitch count 101 x 111

1 Work the cross stitch using two strands throughout. Back stitch the stamens of flowers in two strands of dark lemon and two strands of hunter green for the oval surround. Stitch French knots in dark lemon at the end of each stamen. Back stitch the remaining detail using one strand for each of the following colours: hunter green for the leaves; very dark flesh for the flowers.

2 Wash and iron the work prior to adding the curtain rings. Attach each curtain ring using two strands of hunter green and making two cross stitches over two threads of evenweave. Insert the needle from the back of the fabric and through the curtain ring. Take the needle down though the appropriate hole to make the lower half of the first cross stitch and pass it through the loop on the back. Pull to your normal tension. Complete two full cross stitches and cast off firmly.

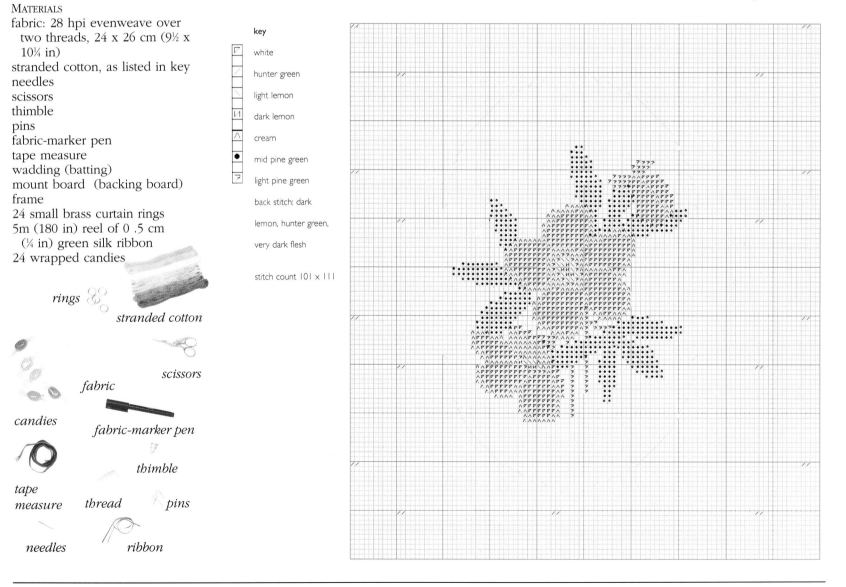

rings
stranded cotton
scissors
fabric
candies
fabric-marker pen
thimble
tape measure _thread_ _pins_
needles _ribbon_

MAKING-UP INSTRUCTIONS

1 Having framed the work, cut 24 pieces ribbon 20.5 cm (8 in) in length, and tie them to the brass rings on the calendar with a small knot.

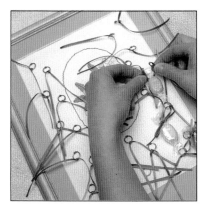

2 Tie a wrapped candy into the bow by first placing the candy onto the knot and then tying a bow over it.

Winter cottage

Winter may seem bleak, but don't despair.
Look around at the distinctive colours of the
season. This cottage brings together all the
glorious tones and hues that denote winter.

YOU WILL NEED

MATERIALS
fabric: 30 hpi linen over two
  threads, 26 x 20 cm
  (10 x 8 in)
stranded cotton, as listed in key
needle
scissors
fabric-marker pen
tape measure
mount board (backing board)
wadding (batting)
pins
thread
frame

fabric

*tape
measure*

*stranded
cotton*

*fabric-
marker
pen*

scissors

needle

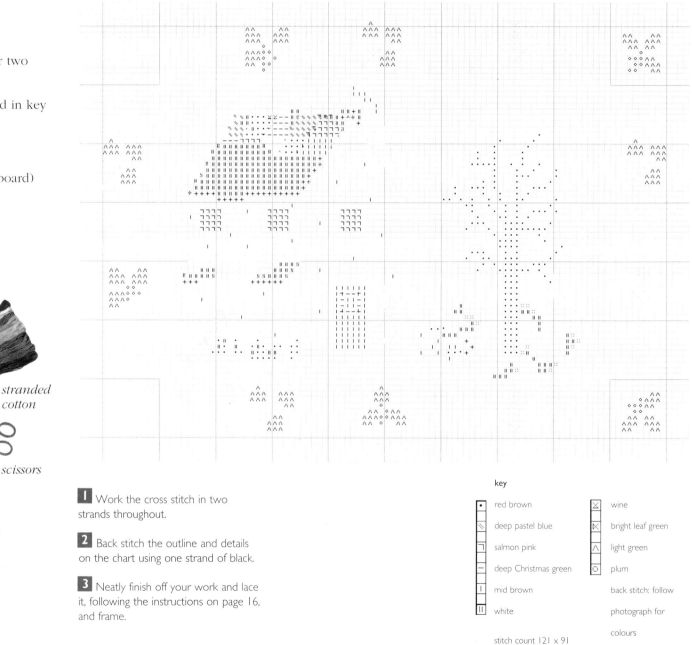

1 Work the cross stitch in two
strands throughout.

2 Back stitch the outline and details
on the chart using one strand of black.

3 Neatly finish off your work and lace
it, following the instructions on page 16,
and frame.

key

•	red brown	⊠	wine
⁄	deep pastel blue	⊠	bright leaf green
⌐	salmon pink	∧	light green
−	deep Christmas green	◦	plum
I	mid brown		back stitch: follow
II	white		photograph for
			colours

stitch count 121 x 91

Robin Christmas stocking

Imagine Santa coming to your home and finding this charming stocking. He'll be sure to fill it full of wonderful treats.

YOU WILL NEED

MATERIALS
fabric: 28 hpi evenweave over
  two threads, 35 x 25 cm
  (14 x 10 in)
stranded cotton, as listed in key
needles
scissors
35 cm (14 in) of contrast fabric
matching thread
lightweight iron-on interfacing
tape measure
20 cm (8 in) of contrast ribbon

fabric

interfacing

contrast fabric

stranded cotton

ribbon

scissors

thread

needle

tape measure

key

•	white
‖	deep coral
=	Christmas red
✳	deep cream
I	mid fern green
╲	black
╱	pearl grey
∧	mahogany
И	mid beige

back stitch: very dark
blue green, very
dark garnet, very
dark mocha brown,
white

stitch count 61 x 71

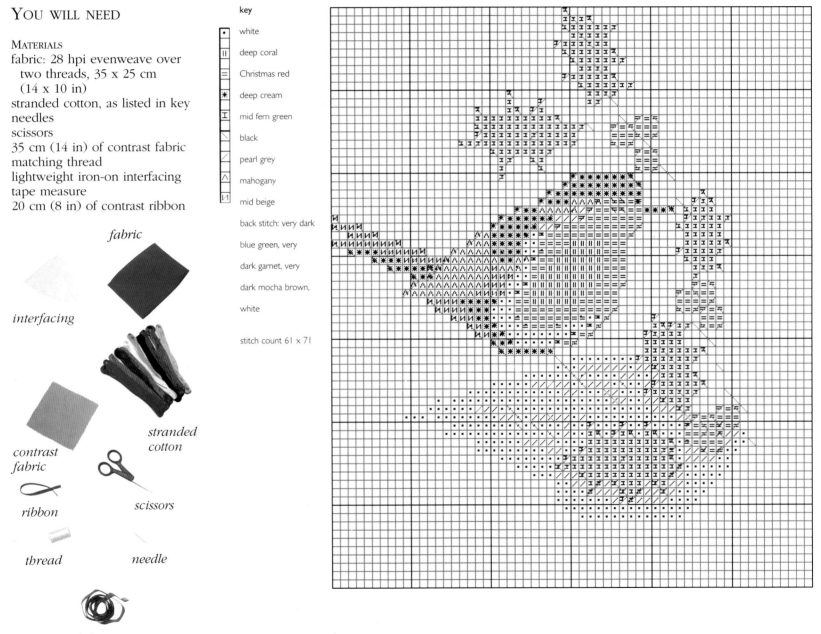

MAKING-UP INSTRUCTIONS

1 Cut out three stocking shapes, one from the evenweave and a pair in contrasting fabric. Position the design in the centre of the evenweave fabric and work the cross stitch using two strands throughout. Back stitch the detail, using one strand, in the following colours: very dark blue green for the leaves and stems; very dark garnet for berries and red breast; very dark mocha brown for the rest of the robin. Use one strand of white for French knots for the eye and on the berries. When the design is complete, iron on lightweight interfacing to the wrong side of the evenweave to reduce fraying.

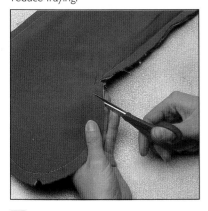

2 Place the evenweave and contrasting fabric stocking pieces right sides together and stitch around the boot and up the sides of the stocking, leaving the top edge open. At the top turn over a 1.5 cm (½ in) hem and stitch around the hem. Turn and press.

SEWING TIP
Never iron directly on to your cross stitch. Always use a dampened cloth over the design to preserve your work.

3 Place remaining contrast fabric stocking right side to embroidered surface of evenweave. Top edge will be approximately 1.5 cm (½ in) above the finished top edge of the front. Stitch around the stocking. Clip curves. Turn right side out and press.

4 Fold a top seam allowance 1.5 cm (½ in) inside stocking and hem, enclosing the hanging ribbon at the back seam.

Christmas tree decoration

A simple flexihoop (embroidery frame) makes a super Christmas tree decoration. Stitch this tree to hang on yours. It's a project which can be attempted by the novice stitcher.

YOU WILL NEED

MATERIALS
fabric: 28hpi evenweave over
  two threads, 11 x 12.5 cm (4½
  x 5 in)
stranded cotton, as listed in key
needle
scissors
flexihoop (frame) 6.5 x 9 cm
  (2½ x 3½ in)
mount board (backing board)
wadding (batting)
pins
felt for backing 11 x 12.5 cm
  (4½ x 5 in)
thread

fabric

*flexihoop
(embroidery
frame)*

felt

needle

*stranded
cotton*

thread

scissors

1 Work the cross stitch using two strands throughout.

2 Back stitch the outline as marked on the chart with one strand of red.

3 Finish the work and place the design in the flexihoop (embroidery frame). Cut the fabric to within one inch of the hoop and sew running stitches around the edge. Pull up the gathers and lace across the back (see page 16). Cut the felt to the same size and stitch the felt to the fabric.

key

✱	red
•	brown
O	green

back stitch: red

stitch count 31 x 41

Bird table

It's not easy for birds in winter. The pickings are poor. Some kind people make their lives more pleasurable by stretching out the hand of generosity and leaving them titbits.

YOU WILL NEED

MATERIALS
fabric: 14 hpi aida, 16.5 x 18 cm
  (6½ x 7 in)
stranded cotton, as listed in key
needle
scissors
tape measure
wadding (batting)
mount board (backing board)
pins
thread
frame

stranded cotton

tape measure

scissors

fabric

wadding (batting)

needle

1 Work the cross stitch using two strands throughout. Use two strands of very light brown for back stitching on branches and lemon for back stitching blackbird's legs and beak.

2 Back stitch remaining detail using one strand for each of the following colours: dark steel grey for chaffinch and blue tit (blue bird); Christmas red for nut bag; black for black bird and footprints; very dark mocha brown for robin, bird table and bread. Use two strands for French knots in lemon for blackbird's eye and black for others.

3 Neatly finish off your work, and lace it, following the instructions on page 16, and frame.

key

•	steel grey
⌐	black
I	Christmas red
−	light peach flesh
+	light tan
÷	lemon
⊠	dark steel grey
⋈	very light brown
∧	light turquoise
И	light yellow beige
⋈	white

⊙	dark mahogany
□	light lemon
↓	pearl grey
←	very dark mocha brown

back stitch: dark steel
grey, Christmas red,
black, very dark mocha
brown, lemon

stitch count 61 x 71

Winter sampler

Mark the occasion by stitching this traditional sampler and make it a Christmas worth remembering.

YOU WILL NEED

MATERIALS
fabric: 28 hpi evenweave over
 two threads, 29 x 36 cm (12 x
 14 in)
stranded cotton, as listed in key
needles
scissors
fabric-marker pen
tape measure
mount board (backing board)
pins
wadding (batting)

1 Work the cross stitch using two strands throughout.

2 Back stitch the detail, using one strand, in the following colours: dark brown for the robin and squirrel's eye, window and door detail; dark beige brown for the twig under robin; mid beige brown for robin's stomach out-line; light steel grey for outline of snow, trees, smoke from chimney. Use three strands for back stitching the robin's legs. Stitch a French knot in dark brown for the door handle.

3 Neatly finish the work. and lace it, following the instructions on page 16, and frame.

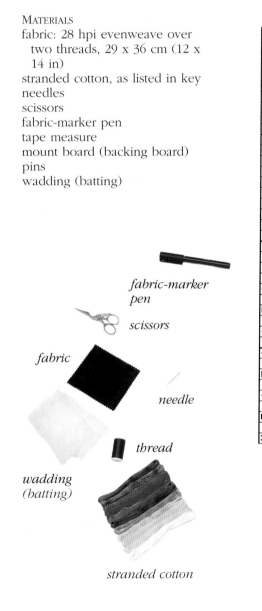

fabric-marker pen

scissors

fabric

needle

thread

wadding (batting)

stranded cotton

	key
•	red
⬚	deep red
⅂	white
–	pearl grey
I	mid brown
II	cream
+	mink brown
⨯	pale grey
⋉	sienna brown
∧	mid olive green
⤧	deep olive green
⠆	Christmas red
○	salmon pink
□	dark beige
↓	dark beige grey
←	dark brown
↖	mocha grey brown
↑	lilac
■	mid salmon
⊥	deep salmon

back stitch: dark
brown, dark beige
brown, mid beige
brown, light steel grey

stitch count 131 x 171

A

Advent calendar, 86
Aida band, 8
Aida tea towel, 8
Aperture (opening) cards, 18
Apple and pears placements, 69
Autumn cottage, 66
Autumn leaves pot stand, 59
Autumn sampler, 74

B

Baby fawn, 31
Back stitch, 14
Beads, 10
Bees and honey tea towel, 72
Bird bookmark, 24
Bird table, 93
Birds in the bath, 21
Blackberry card, 68
Blossom tree, 30
Bookmarks
  bird, 24
  holly, 76
  making, 19
Butterfly gift tags, 43

C

Canvas
  plastic, 8
  waste, 64
Cards
  blackberry, 68
  cottage snow scene, 77
  cyclamen, 81
  filling, 18
  garden, 39
  Halloween pumpkin, 63
  posy of pansies, 20
  Summer house, 50
Chart paper, 8
Chicken tea cosy, 70
Christmas stocking, robin, 90
Christmas tree decoration, 92
Collector's roses, 51
Continuous cross stitch, 12
Cottage snow scene card, 77
Cotton, stranded, 8
Country flowers scissors case, 52
Cross stitch, 12
Cushions
  Autumn, 60
  love, 32
  Spring, 22
  Summer, 40
  Winter, 82
Cyclamen card, 81

D

Daffodil doorstop, 36
Doorplate
  poppy, 38

E

Embroidery frame, 10
Embroider scissors, 10
Equipment, 10

F

Fabric-marker pen, 10
Fabrics, 8
Felt, 8
First snowdrops, 25
Flexihoop. 10
French knots, 15

G

Garden card, 39
Garden fairy, 78
General-purpose scissors, 10
Gift tags
  butterfly, 43
  mistletoe, 80
Glue, 10

H

Half stitch, 13
Halloween pumpkin, 63
Harvest mouse, 64
Hat band
  Summer roses, 46
Holbein stitch, 14
Holly bookmark, 76

I

Interfacing, 8

L

Lacing picture, 16
Lavender bag, 56
Lilac print, 54
Long stitch, 15
Love cushion, 32

M

Masking tape, 10
Materials, 8
Metallic thread, 8
Mistletoe gift tag, 80

N

Napkin
  apple and pears, 69
Napkin holder
  apple and pears, 69

Needles, 10
Nesting squirrel pot, 62
Nightgown case, 26

O

Ornaments, poinsettia, 84

P

Paper, chart, 8
Paperweight
  strawberry, 58
Pictures
  Autumn cottage, 66
  bird table, 93
  birds in the bath, 21
  blossom tree, 30
  lacing, 16
  lilac print, 54
  Spring cottage, 28
  Summer cottage, 44
  Winter cottage, 88
Pinking shears
Pins, 10
Placemats
  apple and pears, 69
Plastic canvas, 8
Poinsettia ornaments, 84
Poppy doorplate, 38
Posy of pansies, 20
Pot stand
  Autumn leaves, 59
Pots
  baby fawn, 31
  decorating, 17
  nesting squirrel pot, 62
  first snowdrops, 25
  Summer garland, 42

Q

Quick unpick (seam ripper), 10

R

Robin Christmas stocking, 90

S

Samplers
  Autumn, 74
  Spring, 34
  Summer, 48
  Winter, 94
Scissors, 10
Scissors case
  country flowers, 52
Sewing thread, 8
Spring cottage, 22
Spring cushion, 28
Spring sampler, 34

Stitches
  back stitch, 14
  continuous cross stitch, 12
  cross stitch, 12
  French knots, 15
  half stitch, 13
  Holbein stitch, 14
  long stitch, 15
  three-quarter stitch, 13
Stranded cotton, 8
Strawberry weight, 58
Summer cottage, 44
Summer cushion, 40
Summer garland, 42
Summer house, 50
Summer roses hat band, 46
Summer sampler, 48

T

Tape measure, 10
Tea cosy
  chicken, 70
Tea towel
  Aida, 8
  bees and honey, 72
Techniques, 12-19
Thimble, 10
Thread, 8
Three-quarter stitch, 13

W

Waste canvas, 8
  working, 64
Winter cottage, 88
Winter cushion, 82
Winter sampler, 94

Publisher's Acknowledgments

The Publisher's are grateful to the following companies who supplied materials used for photography:

Fabric Flair
The Old Brewery, The Close, Warminster, Wiltshire; BA12 9AL. Tel: 01985 846845.
Suppliers of needlecraft fabrics.

Framecraft Miniatures Limited
372/376 Summer Lane, Hockley, Birmingham, B19 3QA. Tel: 0121 212 0551.
Mail order suppliers of frames, miniatures and cards.

Contributors

The Publisher's are grateful to the following contributors whose work appears in this book:

Alison Burton: Apple and pears placemats, napkin holder and napkin; Nightgown case; Poinsettia ornaments; Spring sampler, Winter cushion; Winter sampler.

Sara Creasy: Bees and honey tea towel; Christmas tree decoration; Garden card; Halloween pumpkin.

Lesley Grant: Autumn cushion; Butterfly gift tags; Holly bookmark; Love cushion; Spring cushion; Summer garland.

Rachel Hyde: Chicken tea cosy; Collector's roses; Cottage snow scene; Lavender bag; Summer cushion.

Evelyn King: Mistletoe gift tag; Summer roses.

Julia Tidmarsh: Advent calendar; Autumn leaves pot stand; Baby fawn; Bird table; Birds in the bath; Blackberry card; Blossom tree; Country flowers scissors case; Cyclamen card; First snowdrops; Garden fairy; Harvest mouse; Lilac print, Nesting squirrel; Poppy doorplate; Posy of pansies; Robin Christmas stocking; Strawberry weight; Summer house.

Lynda Whittle: Autumn sampler; Bird bookmark; Daffodil doorstop; Summer sampler.

Dorothy Wood: Autumn cottage; Spring cottage; Summer cottage; Winter cottage.